W9-CQQ-941

HANDBOOK OF DOORMAKING, WINDOWMAKING, AND STAIRCASING

Edited by Antony Talbot

Sterling Publishing Co., Inc.   New York

Publisned in 1980 by
Sterling Publishing Co., Inc.
Two Park Avenue
New York, New York 10016

Library of Congress Catalog Card No.: 79-91389
Sterling ISBN 0-8069-8896-7

Printed in the United States of America

CONTENTS

PREFACE

THE techniques of building finely crafted doors, windows, and staircases appear to be in danger of becoming lost arts. In the name of economy, and in order to compete with mass-produced, machine-made building supplies, builders rarely take the time necessary for refined construction, and the proper methods are taught with less and less frequency. Given the opportunity, most carpenters—and amateurs as well—would gladly learn the methods that allow them to take pride in their work. This handbook provides that opportunity.

There is a growing recognition among the consumer public that those things made well are worth the extra cost involved in their initial production and represent a valuable investment. The minimal amount of extra time and effort involved in producing superior work will be amply repaid by constructions that will last longer, require less maintenance, and perform their functions properly. Furthermore, the enhancement of the quality of a home by the beauty of these well built items cannot be measured in purely monetary terms.

This handbook has been revised and edited from the editions published in the original Woodworker Series of Handbooks. It is reproduced for the benefit of the craftsman woodworker and will provide him with all the information he requires for accurate setting-out and construction. The book will prove to be invaluable to those involved in older-style-house renovation and replacement. It presents the opportunity to add a touch of quality for those who may wish to improve the more modern house.

It is recommended that each of the three sections be read through from beginning to end, as the more complex constructions are based on methods that are fully described only for the simpler designs.

DOORMAKING
For Carpenters and Joiners

DESCRIBING THE DOORS IN ORDINARY USE AND
THE METHOD OF SETTING-OUT AND
CONSTRUCTING THEM

CONTENTS

Doormaking for Carpenters and Joiners

CHAPTER I

VARIOUS TYPES OF DOORS

IN the first place, it is very necessary that crafts-men should learn the correct names of the various patterns of anything in his trade ; we therefore, as a commencement to the present handbook, show sketches and sections of some óf the more commonly used doors, and propose to give the technical terms by which these are generally recognised, following it up later with concise instructions in setting out the required rods and making the doors.

In Figs. 1, 2 and 3 is shown the most easily·made door in use; it is called a " ledge " door in the South of England, but in the North it is a " batten " door.

The front is shown in Fig. 3, and a vertical section in Fig. 2. This kind of door is sometimes made with the ledges close to the outside edge, as at A ; it is then " home-ledged " ; but if they are kept back ½ in., as at B. .it is " back-ledged." Whether made " home-ledged " or " back-ledged " depends upon which way it has to hang in relation to the rebate of the frame, as, if the ledges are towards the rebate, it must be " back-ledged " ; if the other way, " home-ledged."

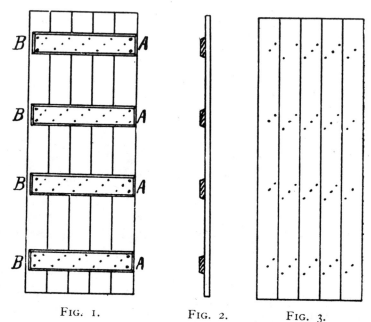

FIG. 1.   FIG. 2.   FIG. 3.

FRONT AND BACK VIEW AND VERTICAL SECTION OF LEDGE
OR BATTEN DOOR.

In the cross-section of the " ledge " door, Fig. 4, are shown various kinds of joints used. C is the

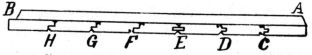

FIG. 4.—CROSS-SECTION OF LEDGE DOOR.

tongue and groove joint, beaded at both sides; D is the same joint, but with one side beaded and the other V-jointed ; E is V-jointed at each side with a loose tongue inserted; F, G, and H are rebated joints—beaded both sides, beaded and V-jointed, and V-jointed both sides respectively.

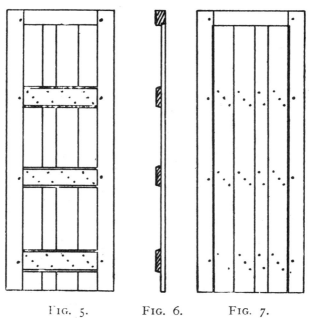

FIG. 5.   FIG. 6.   FIG. 7.

VIEWS AND SECTION OF FRAMED LEDGE DOOR.

In Figs. 5 to 8 are shown the back, face, vertical, and cross sections respectively of a " framed ledge " door in the South, but in the North commonly called a

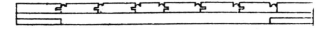

FIG. 8.—CROSS-SECTION OF FRAMED LEDGE DOOR.

" back " door. It is somewhat similar to the ledge door, but has framed stiles and head, the three ledges being tenoned into the stiles, thus making a much stronger door. The space between the stiles is usually filled in with 1-in. match boards, the stiles

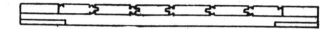

FIG. 9.—CROSS-SECTION OF FRAMED LEDGE DOOR, SHOWING ALTERNATIVE TREATMENT.

being grooved to take the tongues of the two outside boards, and the middle board being cut to width and tongued to fit the extra groove. This method exaggerates the narrow board as shown in Fig. 8, but by the method shown in Fig. 9 the stiles are

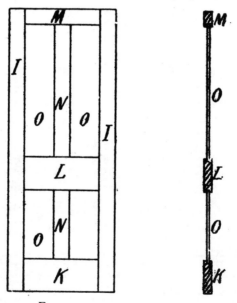

FIG. 10.   FIG. 11.

ELEVATION AND SECTION OF ORDINARY FOUR-PANEL DOOR.

rebated to take the boards, the grooves of the two outer ones being removed and beaded to fit in the rebates ; the finishing board is then cut to width and grooved as required, and by this method the

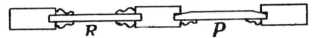

FIG. 12.—SHOWING METHODS OF MOULDING FOUR-PANELLED DOOR.

narrow width of the finishing board is not so apparent, as can be seen in Fig. 9.

Both ledge and framed ledge doors, if very wide, require bracing ; the best methods of doing this will be shown later on.

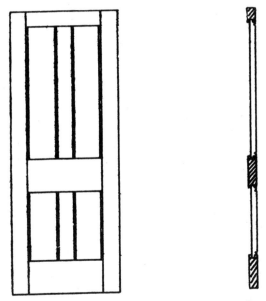

FIG. 13.—BEAD AND BUTT DOOR.

FIG. 15.—SECTION OF BEAD FLUSH DOOR.

Figs. 10 and 11 show the elevation and vertical section of an ordinary four-panel door, consisting of the stiles I, the bottom, middle, and top rails, K, L, and M, the top and bottom muntins N, and the panels O.

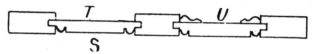

FIG. 14.—SECTION OF BEAD AND BUTT DOOR.

This kind of door is often moulded at one side as P or on both sides as R, Fig. 12 ; it is then styled " moulded and square," or " moulded both sides " respectively, or, in Northern parlance, " planted " on one or both sides.

Fig. 13 is a " bead and butt " door.　The panels are

FIG. 16.—THREE-PANELLED DOOR.

rebated so as to come flush with the stiles at the face side, and a ⅝-in. bead is run down each edge, as shown in section (Fig. 14). In some parts the panel is kept

FIG. 17.—CROSS-SECTION OF BOLECTION-MOULDED DOOR (LOWER PART).

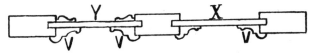

FIG. 18.—CROSS-SECTION OF UPPER PART OF BOLECTION-MOULDED DOOR.

back slightly from the face to save trouble in cleaning off, as at S. These doors can be either " bead butt and square," as T, or " bead butt and moulded," as U.

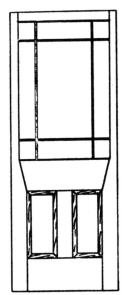

FIG. 19.—ELEVATION OF DIMINISHED STILE DOOR.

" Bead flush " doors are very similar to the above ·

but the bead is mitred quite round the panels, as shown in vertical section in Fig. 15.

In Fig. 16 is shown a three-panelled door with " bolection " moulding and raised bottom panel, a section across the latter being given in Fig. 17, and

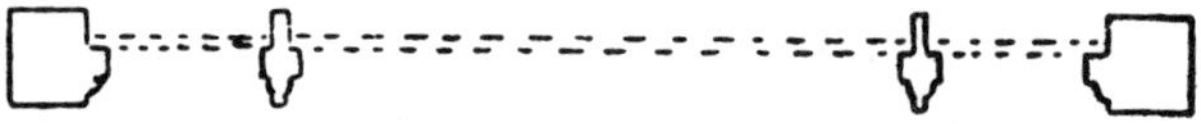

FIG. 20.—CROSS-SECTION OF UPPER PART OF DIMINISHED
STILE DOOR.

another section across the top panels in Fig. 18. V is the " bolection " moulding, W the raised panel, X square inside, and Y moulded inside.

Fig. 19 shows an elevation of a " diminished stile sash door," with moulded bottom panels, and Fig. 20 a section across the top part. The making of this is a combination of door and sash, and presents some pitfalls for the novice, which will, however, be made clear when the proper time comes.

CHAPTER II

CONSTRUCTION OF LEDGE DOORS

ON the principle of beginning at the bottom, we will in the present chapter take in hand the making of the " ledge " door, and what comes next to it in simplicity—the " framed ledge " door.

The former can be dismissed very shortly, the boards and ledges being prepared according to instructions in Chapter I. The whole of the former must be laid, face downwards, either flat on the bench or on two pieces of timber as wide as the ledges. They are then cramped up fairly tightly, and the ledges laid on them. The top and bottom ones of these must be fixed first, squaring them across at about 5 ins. from the respective ends of the door, and fixing them at each end with two screws in each. The intermediate ledges are then fixed in the same way, keeping them at equal distances between. A single nail can now be driven through two of the ledges into the middle board (to prevent the boards from springing out), and the door turned over. The position of the four ledges must now be squared across on the top side, as the door lies, as a guide for nailing.

Two methods of nailing are shown in Fig. 21. That shown at A is favoured by a good many, but (B) is preferred, as not being so liable to split the ledges, and also as acting more as a brace.

When all of the nails are driven in, they should be sunk still further by punching; the door can then be turned over and the nails clinched neatly, also using the punch.

The screws in the ends of the ledges (Fig. 22) are sometimes omitted, but this is a mistake, as they add very much to the strength of the door. Another mistake often made is the use of too long nails— 2-in. nails are long enough for a 1-in. door, $2\frac{1}{2}$-in. nails for $1\frac{1}{4}$-in. door, and so on.

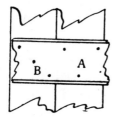

FIG. 21.—METHODS OF NAILING.

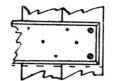

FIG. 22.—END OF LEDGE, SHOWING SCREWS.

We now come to the important matter of bracing, which is necessary for all doors over $2\frac{1}{2}$ ft. wide. The usual method is to brace them as Fig. 23, notching the ledges to form abutments for the ends of the braces; but after testing the matter in various ways, it has been found that a door braced as Fig. 24 will keep its position far better than one braced the other way, while it is far easier, more quickly done, takes less material, and presents a better appearance—consequently it should always be adopted.

As will be seen by Fig. 24, the braces are simply cut between the ledges, and fixed by nails or screws ; the latter should at least be used at the ends.

We now come to the framed ledged door, which was sufficiently described in Chapter I to enable anyone to recognise it without further description. We can therefore presume that the framing is planed up and the boards prepared, and will proceed at once

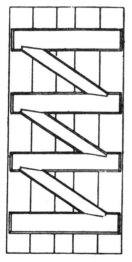 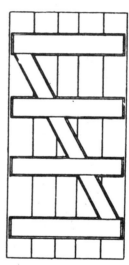

FIG. 23.—USUAL METHOD OF BRACING.   FIG. 24.—ALTERNATIVE METHOD OF BRACING.

to set out the door. This requires a " setting-out rod," on which is marked the full size, with every mortise, tenon, bead, rebate, etc., and this rod is shown in Fig. 25 (A). The full height of the door is from C to D. E is the mortise for top rail ; F the haunching for same ; G the mortises for the ledges ; H the space from bottom of door to bottom ledge ; and I the spaces between the ledges, which must be all equal.

To set out the stiles, lay them face to face on the bench, and lay the rod on them, so that the lines can

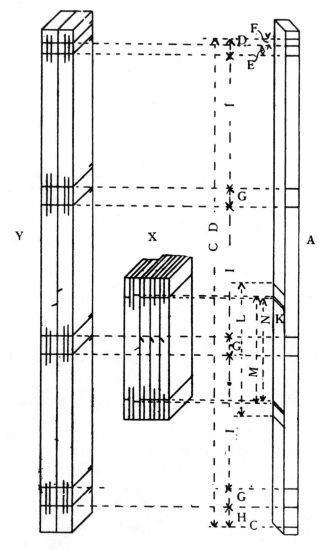

FIG. 25.—SETTING-OUT ROD, WITH RAILS AND STILES MARKED OFF.

be transferred from the one to the other, as shown by dotted lines from A to Y, Fig. 25, which latter show all mortises squared over and wedging marked, also gauging for mortises.

The width of the door is set out on the rod at **K**, the finished width being shown by L, the length from shoulder to shoulder on the face side of top rail at **M**, and the length of the back shoulder of top rail,

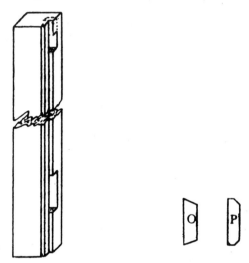

FIG. 26.—STILE FOR FRAMED   FIG. 27.—SECTIONS SHOWING
        LEDGE DOOR.   BEVEL ON LEDGES.

and the shoulders of bare-faced tenons on the ledges at N (see dotted lines).

The three ledges and top rail are shown set out and gauged for cutting at X, Fig. 25. Perhaps it will be as well to state that the ledges are gauged with a marking gauge, set to the correct thickness of the tenon required.

One stile is shown mortised, rebated, and beaded

(the haunching is shown by dotted lines) in Fig. 26, while Fig. 27 shows sections of the ledges bevelled in two different ways. O is bevelled quite through, for which the mortises should be bevelled as well, while P is bevelled on only as far as the tenons, thus requiring square mortises only.

Fig. 28 shows the back of the complete door, braced as recommended for the ledge door. The

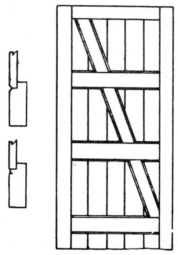

FIG. 28.—BACK OF FRAMED LEDGE DOOR, WITH SECTIONS OF TOP RAIL AND BOARDS.

brace at the top end should be kept on the top rail ; if it goes to the stile, it has a tendency to force it off, as anyone may see, if he will take notice of any doors where the brace is fixed into the angle formed by the stile and the top rail.

It is sometimes necessary to make a door in two parts, to be hinged one above the other. Such a door is shown in Fig. 29, A being a vertical section, where it will be seen that the top door shuts into a bevelled rebate, made in the top rail of the bottom door.   B shows a vertical section of a similar pair of doors ; but the bottom ledge of the top door is brought down and fits closely on the top rail of the bottom door.   C is a section of ordinary ledge doors hung in two parts to answer the same pur-

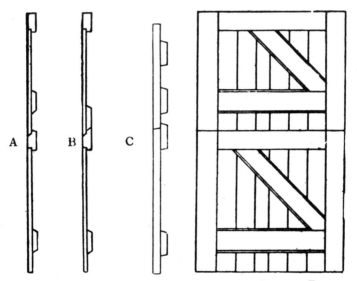

FIG. 29.—ELEVATION AND SECTIONS OF LEDGE DOOR IN TWO PARTS.

pose, the top ledge of the bottom door projecting above the boards, so as to form a rebate for the top door.

When hingeing doors such as these, the top one must be hung so as to throw up considerably, or they will bind in opening.

Fig. 30 is a cross-section of folding ledge doors; the strip R being screwed on to one door to cover the joint.

Fig. 31 is a cross-section of folding framed ledge doors, the two meeting stiles being rebated together and beaded as at S.

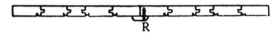

R

FIG. 30.—SECTION OF FOLDING LEDGE DOORS.

Fig. 32 shows a cross-section of a rough ledge door, in which square jointed boards are used, the strips being nailed up the joints instead of tongues. This

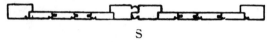

S

FIG. 31.—SECTION OF FOLDING FRAMED LEDGE DOORS.

kind of door is often used for sheds and farm buildings, and somewhat rarely in cottages.

One more word as to bracing doors. The brace

FIG. 32.—SECTION OF ROUGH LEDGE DOOR.

should always be at the bottom of the door on the *hanging* side, so that it is. in compression, not in tension.

CHAPTER III

A Four-Panelled Door

THE subject of the present chapter is, perhaps, easier to make than any other variety ; but, at the same time, it should be done properly, if a good result is to follow.

Panel doors are, as a rule, made in certain stock sizes, such as 6 ft. 4 ins. by 2 ft. 4 ins., 6 ft. 6 ins. by 2 ft. 6 ins., 6 ft. 8 ins. by 2 ft. 8 ins., and so on ; although, at times, odd sizes are required.

The first thing to be done is to face up the stuff properly, as we have described in previous chapters, and preferably to gauge it to thickness, and the next item is to set out the " rod." This latter is shown at A (Fig. 33), the height of the door being set out on the side B, and the width on C. The full height of the door is first marked off on the rod, as D D, then the distance from bottom of door to the top of the middle rail (which is usually 3 ft. 1 in.) as D E ; again from E downwards for width of the middle rail E F, and upwards from D for width of the bottom rail D G, and lastly from the top D downwards for width of the top rail D H.

Now set out from F and H upwards and from E and G downwards ½ in., as shown, this being the depth of the panel grooves, and from the latter marks set off for the mortises J and haunchings K ; the two

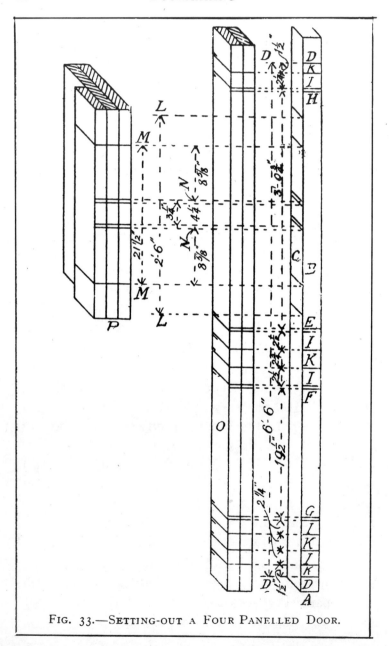

FIG. 33.—SETTING-OUT A FOUR PANELLED DOOR.

former (if 9-in. rails are used) should be 2¼ ins., and the latter 2¼ ins. and 1½ ins., respectively.

The top rail is divided into mortise and haunching in the same way ; also the middle rail, the mortises in the latter being made 2½ ins. wide.

The width of the door is marked off as L L, and the width of the stiles set back from it as M M. The centre between these is then found and the width of

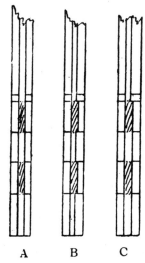

A   B   C

FIG. 34.—SHOWING VARIOUS WIDTHS OF GROOVES.

the muntin set off from this as N N, the two marks half an inch from the latter giving the width of the mortises required.

Now to set out the stiles. Lay them on the bench face to face, with the squared edges towards you, and with the rod on the top of them. Then with the square transfer the marks from the one to the other, as shown by the dotted lines in Fig. 33. The lines for the mortises must then be squared across the top as at O and down on the back edges, also the additional lines for the wedging as shown.

The lines, E, F, G, and H, are simply guide lines; the mortise lines are the ones half an inch from them.

FIG. 35.—BOTTOM RAIL OF FOUR-PANELLED DOOR.

To set out the rails, lay them on the bench in the same way as the stiles as at P, and transfer the shoulder lines to the edges as shown ; also the mortise and guide lines for the muntins. The latter can be done with a pencil, but the shoulder lines should be cut with knife or chisel. These latter must be squared across on both sides, but with the exception of the middle rail the mortises do not require this.

The muntins must now be set out by transferring

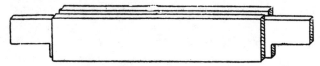

FIG. 36.—TOP RAIL OF FOUR-PANELLED DOOR.

the marks F and G and E and H to the bottom and top muntins respectively, keeping them slightly full in length to ensure a close fit.

The mortise gauge should be set to the chisel which comes nearest to a third of the thickness of the stuff—

thus the 7-16ths and the 9-16ths will be as a rule correct for 1½-in. and 1¾-in. doors respectively, and in most cases the mortises should be made in the middle. It sometimes happens that owing to the stuff not holding up to thickness, or from the moulding being thicker than usual (if the doors have to be

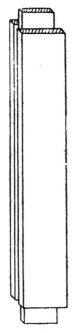 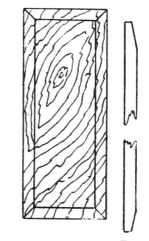

Fig. 37.—Muntin of Four-panelled Door.

Fig. 38.—Back of Panel, and Section.

moulded), that it is necessary to throw the mortises more to one side, to make room for the moulding, of which more hereafter.

The whole of the setting out and gauging being done, the mortises should be made and cleaned out, also the tenons cut, but not the shoulders; this having to be left until the ploughing is done, which comes next.

The general rule is to use the same width of plough iron as mortise chisel, and this should always be done, providing that the panels to be used hold up to the requisite thickness to fill the grooves, and that there will be room for the moulding ; if moulded doors are in hand.

If, then, this rule is followed out, the edge of the stile when mortised and ploughed will be as A, Fig. 34. If, however, thin panels are to be used, or extra room made for moulding, a smaller iron must be used for ploughing, so that the edge of the stile will be

FIG. 39.—PANEL IN FRAMING, MOULDED ONE SIDE.

as B, and in this case the grooves between the mortises must be brought out to the width of the latter to make room for the haunchings, so that the appearance will be as C.

The grooving done, the shoulders must next be cut, using a tenon saw, and cutting *up to* the mark, not *on* it ; after which the haunchings must be cut out, not as solid pieces, but as wedges to use in wedging up the door when done.

The appearance of the bottom rail, the top rail, and the muntins, after the shoulders and haunchings are cut, is as Figs. 35, 36, and 37, respectively. The tenons on the latter need not be more than 2 ins. long.

The skeleton of the door should now be fitted

together, so as to be certain that all shoulders will come up properly, and, if all is correct, the panels can be prepared.

These should be cut off about 1-16th in. shorter than the space they have to fill (panel space plus depth of grooves), and also cut so much less in width, before anything else is done to them ; they can then be faced up and planed to the right thickness to fit the grooves—first the ends, then the sides, or as it is called in technical language, " mulletted," and then the back planed off. If the door is to be left square, or only moulded one side, the panels are left as mulletted, as in Fig. 38, and, in position in the door,

FIG. 40.—PANEL IN FRAMING, MOULDED BOTH SIDES.

in Fig. 39; but if to be moulded both sides, the bevel on the back of the panels must be planed off level, as in Fig. 40.

The door should now be taken apart, so as to get the panels in, and all the joints knocked up to make certain that the panels are neither too long nor too wide ; and if it is correct, the stiles should be knocked off, as in Fig. 41, the tenons well glued on both sides and cramped up again, the wedges glued and driven in and left till the glue is dry, when it can be cleaned off and moulded if required. This latter operation is simple ; the moulding is cut the right length to fit the panels and nailed in—not into the panels, but into the stiles, as shown in Figs. 39 and 40.

FIG. 41.—DOOR READY FOR GLUEING.

In some shops it is the rule not to glue the tenons, and I am afraid that some omit to glue the wedges as well ; but if the work is to be done properly, the tenons and the wedges must be glued—and glued well.

If two or more doors are in hand at the same time, they should all be set out together, taking care to keep the stiles in pairs, also the rails ; and if, say, half-a-dozen pairs of stiles have to be set out at once, it is best to set out one pair first, and lay one of these at the top and the other at the bottom of the pile. They will then correct any tendency of the square to be out of truth, when squaring down the edges.   The above also applies to the rails—even more particularly than to the stiles.

In cutting off stuff for panel doors, 3 ins. extra should be allowed in the length of the stiles, and $\frac{1}{2}$ in. in the rails—the latter to allow for cleaning off, and the former to prevent the wedges from splitting the haunchings.

Panel doors are sometimes described as "batten," " deal," and " plank " framing, meaning that 7-in., 9-in., or 11-in. rails, and 3½-in., 4½-in., and 5½-in. stiles, top rails, and muntins, respectively are used.

CHAPTER IV

Bead Butt and Bead Flush Doors

The general rules as regards the dimensions of these doors, also width of stiles and rails, etc., are the same as in the ordinary panel doors, described in the previous chapter. Thus it follows that the method of setting out is somewhat similar. At the same time more careful work is required, as we shall show later on.

The rod for setting out is shown in Fig. 42, A being the height, and B the width, and in the same figure is shown the pair of stiles, set out and gauged ready for mortising; also the bottom, middle, and top rails, set out from the rod, squared over for the shoulders, and gauged for tenoning.

The illustration also shows the bottom muntins and panels and the top ditto (C being the muntins, and D the panels), set out, and shoulders squared across, also gauged for tenons and tongues.

So far the setting out is a repetition of what has gone before; but with the panels comes a new phase, and one which requires care. First, as to the thickness of the panels. These, having to come flush with the door on the " face " side, must be considerably thicker than those described before; thus, for $1\frac{1}{2}$-in., $1\frac{3}{4}$-in., and 2-in. doors, the panels must be 1 in., $1\frac{1}{4}$ ins., and $1\frac{1}{2}$ ins., thick respectively, that is, they should be (it does not follow that they

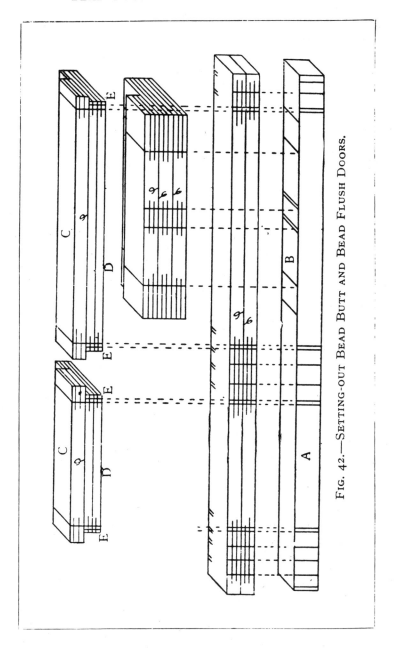

FIG. 42.—SETTING-OUT BEAD BUTT AND BEAD FLUSH DOORS.

always are so). Therefore, in setting the gauge for
the mortises, the thickness of the panels must be
worked to in the first instance, and the size of the
mortise arranged accordingly.

Another thing in connection with the panels
has to do with the setting out, which should, if
possible, be done in conjunction with the setting
out of the muntins, as C and D, Fig. 42.   It is

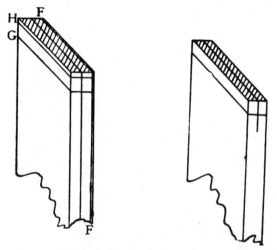

FIGS. 43 AND 44.—MARKING-OUT TONGUES ON ENDS
OF PANELS.

imperative that the shoulders of the muntins coincide
exactly with the shoulders of the panels, which they
will do if both are set out at one and the same time.

The dead length of the panels is the distance
between the mortises in the stiles, as shown by the
dotted lines.   Thus it will be understood that the
small pieces at E are simply waste, and represent
the squaring off of the panels.

The proper way, to prepare the panels is to first

face up the best side, and reduce to the correct width. Then run the mortise gauge all round, as in Fig. 43. This shows that the panel requires planing down to the mark F.   After this set out the panels, and square across for dead length and shoulders, as at G and H.   The panels are now cut off at the mark H, and the gauge run along the ends again, when they will be as Fig. 44, and ready for sawing in at the

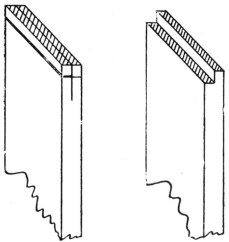

FIGS. 45 AND 46.—CUTTING TONGUES ON ENDS OF PANELS.

shoulders, which in Fig. 45 is shown as done, while in Fig. 46 the waste has been cut out to the gauge line and the tongue formed.

The next operation is to rebate the sides to form the tongues, and this is done in Fig. 47, while in Fig. 48 the two beads have been run and the panel finished. The regulation size of the beads on the panels is $\frac{5}{8}$ in., although in rare cases $\frac{1}{2}$ in. only is used.

The advantages of preparing the panels as above are :—the "face" side will always come flush with the framing, so as to need very little cleaning off ; the tongues will always fit as they should do, being gauged to the same size as the plough iron ; and any waste which is planed off the panels is taken off the worst side of the panel instead of the best, which is the case when the inside is prepared first.

We are induced to make these explanations owing

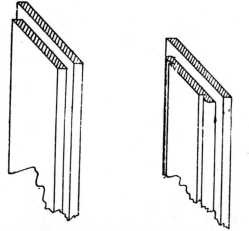

FIGS. 47 AND 48.—REBATING AND BEADING PANELS.

to our being fully aware that a great many do not work by this method, and thus to disarm criticism ; but after following the method for many years ourselves, we are certain it is the best, both in theory and practice.

The door is now ready for putting together ; but it is as well to make sure it will not be panel-bound, to take a shaving or two off the panels all round.

And it would perhaps be well to mention that in taking the panels to a width, as well as when rebating them at the sides, as Fig. 47, to allow about a thirty-second

FIG. 49.—MEETING OF PANEL AND RAIL.

FIG. 50.—SECTION OF MUNTIN AND PANELS.

part of an inch clearance, as panels are apt to swell, and if made too tight at first will force the shoulders of the door apart.

The actual process of putting together and glueing up the door is the same as described in Chapter III, and need not be repeated here. The

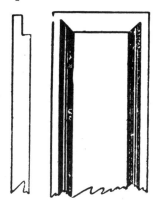
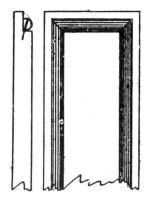

FIG. 51.—PANEL OF BEAD FLUSH DOOR, WITH SECTION.

FIG. 52.—PANEL COMPLETED, AND SECTION SHOWING BEAD BRADDED IN.

cleaning off can also be passed over ; but it will be found that a neat touch and sharp plane is necessary to make a good job of the panels where they butt up to the rails, as in Fig. 49. The sides will present no difficulty, as the bead will form a division between the two, as shown in section, Fig. 50.

In making the bead flush doors, the procedure is the same as for bead butt, until the panels are finished, as Fig. 48, after which they must be cut back at each end, mitreing the beads, as Fig. 51 (and in section at A), and a length of $\frac{5}{8}$-in. bead fitted and bradded in, as in Fig. 52. The panels can then be put in the door, and the latter glued up and cleaned off in the usual way.

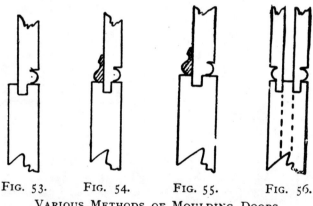

FIG. 53.   FIG. 54.   FIG. 55.   FIG. 56.
VARIOUS METHODS OF MOULDING DOORS.

The cleaning off of a bead flush door is much easier than a bead butt, owing to the beads forming a break in the level surface. The difficulty of the latter is, however, in some parts met by using slightly thinner panels, and keeping them back from the face of the door, thus economising both material and labour to a certain extent, but at the same time it spoils the appearance of the door.

The finished door can be either " bead butt and

square," as Fig. 53, or " bead butt and moulded," as Fig. 54; the same, of course, applying to bead flush doors. Fig. 55 is a section of a " bead butt and moulded " door, with panels set back as described.

In Fig. 56 is shown part section of a double bead butt (or bead flush) door. In this case thinner panels are used, and the grooves kept clear of the mortises, the latter being made as shown by the dotted lines.

Figs. 57, 58, and 59 show section and part elevation of " bead and centre bead butt," " reeded butt," and " moulded butt " panels respectively, the two latter can also be used for flush doors as well if required.

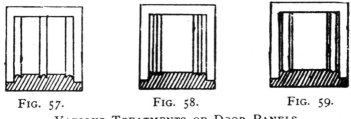

FIG. 57.   FIG. 58.   FIG. 59.

VARIOUS TREATMENTS OF DOOR PANELS.

The method of making will be the same as those already described ; therefore, there is no necessity to dwell further on them.

The " bead butt " and " bead flush " doors are largely used in some parts for front doors, being only intended for outside doors, the panels being kept flush to allow the wet to run off them ; and as they are common in some parts, and quite unknown in others, we will in the next chapter deal with the various kinds of outside doors which are used as substitutes in those parts which do not recognise the " bead butt."

CHAPTER V

Two- and Three-Panelled Doors, etc

THE door shown in Fig. 60 is very common as a front door in some parts of the country, although it has not much to recommend it, the long panels being very weak, and also the stiles, owing to there being no middle rail to strengthen them.

The making is very simple, being the same as an ordinary panel door, minus the middle rail; hence no detailed instructions in setting out are required here. The only mystifying point is the circular head panels, but these are only formed by the bolection moulding, the top rail being framed in square, as in Fig. 61, and the circular corner pieces glued and bradded in on the outside of the door only,

The circular moulding is formed in a lathe, as Fig. 62, and cut through to form the two heads. It should be sawn through across the grain, as shown in the drawing, so that the end grain on the straight mould-ing will butt against the end grain on the circular moulding. By doing this, the shrinkage will be the same on each piece, and the intersection will not be affected. Of course, it must be understood that, if a good job is to be made, the turning must be accurately done, or the two will not intersect, and no amount of cleaning off will put matters right.

In making doors which have to be bolection moulded, some care is needed in gauging for the mortises, to ensure the moulding bedding properly. If the moulding is rebated to a depth of half an inch, the gauge should be set to nine-sixteenths ; the moulding will then bed tightly on 1he framing without any

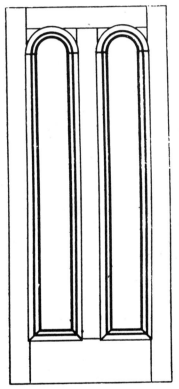

FIG. 60.—TWO-PANELLED DOOR.

trouble. If gauged on too far, when the moulding is nailed in there is a risk of splitting at the outside edge ; and if not gauged far enough, the moulding will not fit closely to the framing. The medium should be aimed at, as in Fig. 63, where the moulding beds closely at A and B, and is slightly away from the panel at C.

In fitting bolection moulding, the mitres should be shot. as it is difficult to obtain a clean joint direct

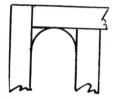

FIG. 61.—SHOWING CORNER-PIECES IN PANELS.

FIG. 62.—CIRCULAR MOULD-ING FOR TOPS OF PANELS.

from the saw ; the correct length of each piece should be taken, and the moulding cut to the marks ; there will then be no difficulty in making them fit accurately. The rebates are usually made slightly wedge-shaped, as shown in Fig. 63, which forces the mitres up tightly as the mouldings are driven in. In nailing each piece in, the nails should be driven as at D (Fig. 63) ; this will draw the points A and B down tightly, and

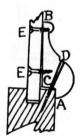

FIG. 63.—METHOD OF FIXING BOLECTION MOULDING.

at the same time allow the panels to shrink, without the danger of splitting them. This method of fixing does not, however, find favour in some parts, the favourite method being to screw the moulding from the

inside of the panels, as at E. This certainly holds
them firmly to the panels; but unless the latter are
very dry, they are apt to split, owing to the outside
edges being held by the screws. Taken on the whole,

FIG. 64.—BOLECTION-MOULDED THREE-PANEL DOOR (WITH
SECTION).

the former method of fixing is preferred, and it must
be understood that both methods should on no
account be used together.

In Fig. 64 we have a door which will be a familiar
object to some readers, but a total stranger to others :

it is a bolection-moulded three-panel door, the third panel being formed by leaving out the bottom muntin, and throwing the whole space below the middle rail into one panel.   This, however, is relieved by planting on a raised panel of ¾-in. wood, bevelled off from the centre to all four sides to a thickness of ⅜ in. and screwed to the panel proper from the inside.

A vertical section of such a door is also shown, and an enlarged section of the bottom part appears in Fig. 65.   In some cases a narrow raised panel is fixed to the upper panels in the same way as the lower, but this is not commonly done.

The above makes a very substantial good-looking door when finished, far better than that shown in

FIG. 65.—ENLARGED DETAIL OF FIG. 64.

Fig. 60; but to ensure lasting properties the bottom panels should be very dry, and the grain should cross in the two—that is, the panel proper should run longways, and the raised panel upright, or *vice-versa*.

Fig. 66 is a bolection-moulded door with glass or lead lights in the upper panels : this also is a localised style of door, and is not often met with. It is, however, a very fair specimen of a front door, and deserves to be more widely known.

The only novelty consists in the method of fitting the glass or lights without stopping the grooves, these being ploughed through as though for ordinary panels. This is done by fitting strips in the grooves, as Figs. 67 and 68, with the rebate side toward the inside of the door, the edge of the strip coming level with the edge of the bolection.

The inside moulding must also come level with these, so that this will hold the glass or lights in position

FIG. 66.—BOLECTION-MOULDED DOOR, WITH LIGHTS IN UPPER PANELS (WITH SECTION).

these fitting in the rebate made for them in the strips. As the inside moulding has to be removed each time new glass is required, it should be screwed in position, in preference to the usual bradding, and to ensure close contact between the strips and the bolection moulding, they also should be screwed together—from the inside, of course.

Fig. 66 shows a vertical section of the complete door, and Fig. 68 an enlarged section of the glass panels and bolection moulding.

It is often the case that mortise locks are inserted

FIG. 67.—REBATED STRIP.   FIG. 68.—SECTION OF GLASS
                                  PANELS AND MOULDINGS.

in panel doors, and if these are tenoned as usual the wedging is entirely cut away in the mortise made for the lock. To obviate this, it is best at any time when it is known that mortise locks will be used, and which way the door will be hung, to use double tenons at the middle rail on the lock side. The setting out of these is shown in Fig. 69; the inner lines are made by the gauge in the ordinary way, as for the usual mortise; another gauge is then set to make the outside lines, the mortise for the lock being eventually

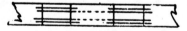

FIG. 69.—SETTING-OUT FOR MORTISE LOCK.

made, as dotted lines. This, however, must not be done till after the door is glued up and set hard. Before putting the door together, the middle rail should be mortised for the lock, between the tenons, as this is much easier to do at this stage than after the door is finished.

CHAPTER VI

A DIMINISHED STILE SASH DOOR

THE diminished stile sash door is so-called on account of the stiles being reduced in width at the upper— or sash—part of the door, thus giving a lighter and neater appearance, and also giving room for more glass. Such doors are often used in vestibules and similar situations, and, although at first sight they seem very simple to make, they do not come so in practice, especially to the novice.

Following our usual plan, we—in Figs. 70 and 71 —show the elevation, with vertical and horizontal sections respectively of the complete door, and in Fig. 72 is the rod, set out with mortises and shoulder lines, ready for transferring to the various parts of the door. But, before doing so, we must explain in detail the best way to prepare the stiles for setting out. It is obvious that, on account of the reduced width of the stiles, it is impossible to square the mortises from the face edge in the usual way. We therefore use the back or outside edges of the stiles as the face, carefully gauging the two parts (top and bottom) to a parallel width from them, so that the lines, being at right angles to the outside edges, will also be the same from the insides.

The mortises on the rod are marked A, and the haunchings B, and these must be squared across from rod to stiles, as shown by dotted lines, to C,

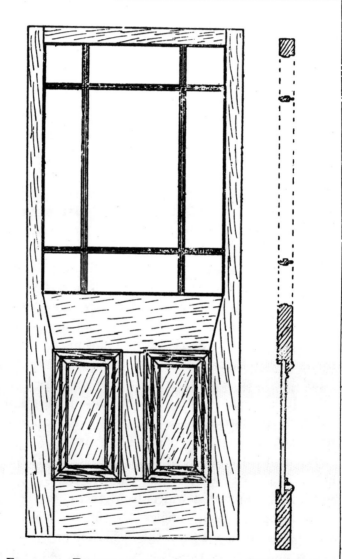

FIG. 70.—ELEVATION AND SECTION OF DIMINISHED STILE DOOR.

It will be noticed that the bottom part of the door is the same as the ordinary panel door, and the mortises come $\frac{1}{2}$ in. from the edges of the rails ; but the top part is different, the mortises coming to the extreme edges of the middle and top rails, also the bars : these latter, therefore, should be marked with the setting-out knife or chisel to ensure perfect fitting.

In gauging for the mortises, the gauge should be set so that the mortise just fills the square between the moulding and the rebate on the sash part of the door. This can be made to suit the width of the mortise chisel by regulating the width of the rebate to suit.

FIG. 71.—SECTION OF UPPER PART OF DIMINISHED STILE DOOR.

The two upright sash bars will be set out from the height rod the same as the stiles (D, Fig. 72), with the exception of the mortises : these are not wanted on the bars, their place being taken by the two lines, as shown, the distance apart of which is regulated by the thickness of the tongues on the bars.

The width of the door is set out on the left side of the rod—the upper end being the sash part of the door, and the lower part of the panelled portion.

The middle and top rails, also the two cross-bars, are shown as set out at E. The shoulders must be left long enough to fit into the rebates and mouldings, as shown by the dotted lines.

The top rail does not need mortising through

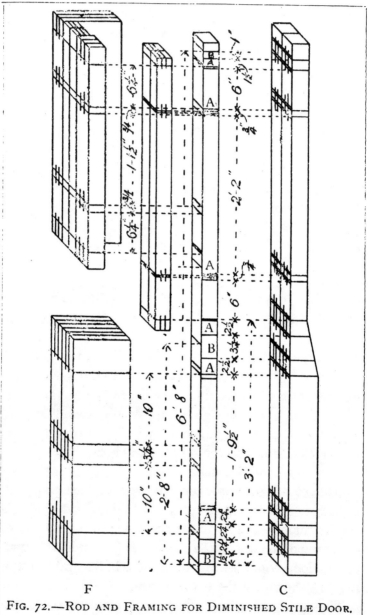

FIG. 72.—ROD AND FRAMING FOR DIMINISHED STILE DOOR.

but to the depth of 1 in. only, and the middle rail will
not need squaring across for the shoulders, as these
have to be on the bevel. to fit the diminishing stiles.

The setting out of the middle and bottom rails for
the bottom portion of the door is shown at F, Fig. 72 ;
but, as this is the same as an ordinary door, it should
not require any explanation.

The best way to mark the diminishing stiles and
the corresponding shoulders on the middle rail is by
means of a pair of templates, as Fig. 73, C for the

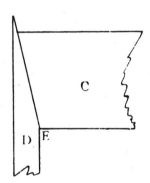

FIG. 73.—TEMPLATES FOR
MARKING-OUT SHOULDERS.

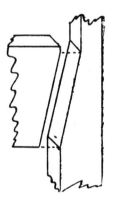

FIG. 74.—DIMINISHING
PART OF STILE.

rails and D for the stiles. If these are made to fit
together so that the angle at E is a perfect right
angle, no trouble will be experienced in making the
shoulders fit.

There is one little thing in connection with the
middle rail which needs mentioning ; this is what
has, with some truth, been called the beginner's
trap. It is this : the stiles should not be diminished
until the whole width of the rail will fit to them ;

but the depth of the moulding less, the rail being
cut to correspond, as in Fig. 74. The stiles will be
still further diminished on working the moulding and
rebating, and the rail will fit ; whereas, if the former
were diminished so as to take the full width of the

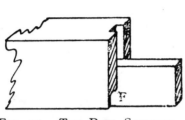

FIG. 75.—TOP RAIL SCRIBED
AND HAUNCHED.

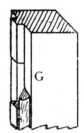

FIG. 76.—TOP
OF STILE.

latter at the beginning, the moulding on the rail
would not meet the other as it should do, but would
leave space between. A very good object-lesson can
be had by making a joint such as this for trial.

The top rail must be haunched as Fig. 75, and the
moulding cut away (" scribed ") to fit that on the
stiles, as at F. The moulding on the stiles is cut

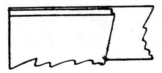

FIG. 77.—HOW TO CUT THE MIDDLE RAIL.

away, as at G, Fig. 76, to allow the square part of the
shoulder to fit in.

The moulding on the middle rail is cut out in the
same way as in Fig. 77, while Fig. 78 shows how
to " scribe " the bars.

The upright bars are first sawn in at the shoulders, as Fig. 79, and after moulding and rebating (technically " sticking "), they are sawn asunder as Fig. 80, first numbering each portion.

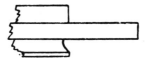

FIG. 78.—HOW TO SCRIBE THE BARS.

These are then " scribed " as at H, and on putting them into the cross bars, the joint in section is as Fig. 81—I being the cross-bar, and K the two portions of the upright bar.

It must be understood that all mortises must be

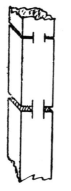

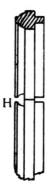

FIG. 79.—UPRIGHT BARS SAWN
AT SHOULDERS.

FIG. 80.—UPRIGHT BARS
MOULDED AND SAWN
ASUNDER.

made and all tenons cut before moulding and rebating ; but not the shoulders ; with the exception of the shoulders on the bars, these should be cut, and not the tenons : these taking the whole of the width between the moulding and rebate, are formed by cutting away the latter with the chisel, after " sticking." It will be noticed that the thickness of the various portions of the door is shown out of pro-

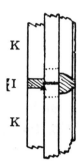

FIG. 81.—METHOD OF JOINTING BARS.

portion in Fig. 72. This is done for the sake of showing the gauge lines clearly ; to show the width of each part in proportion would occupy too much space.

CHAPTER VII

THE MARGINAL STILED DOOR

THE style of door which we intend to describe in this chapter will probably come as a novelty to some readers, while to others it will appear familiar, it being, to a large extent, confined to certain districts. It might, however, with advantage be introduced in many places where it is at present unknown.

As seen by the elevation in Fig. 82, this door has the appearance of a pair of folding doors when closed, and as these are used principally where a single door is not wide enough to fill a given space, so the marginal stiled door is made use of in the same way in places where a wide door is wanted, but not of such a height as to correspond. Thus, a door of 4 ft. wide by 6 ft. 6 ins. high, made in the ordinary way, would look decidedly out of proportion ; whereas, if made with marginal stiles, the appearance is quite as it should be, the alteration being caused by the double stiles in the middle in place of the muntins in ordinary doors.

The construction of these doors varies little from the ordinary panel door, with the exception of the middle stiles ; it is to these, therefore, that we shall pay particular attention.

As stated above, the elevation of the complete door is given in Fig. 82, and a cross-section in Fig. 83 ; the latter, however, shows one side as bolection

FIG. 82.—ELEVATION OF MARGINAL STILED DOOR.

moulded, and the other as bead butt, these doors being suitable for either variety.

The height rod is shown in Fig. 84 B and the four stiles in Fig. 84 C, set out from the rod, and it is to these two figures that we must call particular attention. It will be noticed that in addition to the mortises for the bottom, middle, and top rails, there are two other mortises—one near the bottom, and the other near the top rail at A A. These two mortises must be set out on the two inner stiles only, and they are intended for the reception of hardwood tongues, which form the means of holding the two stiles together. One point to be taken notice of is

FIG. 83.—CROSS-SECTION OF MARGINAL STILED DOOR.

this : whereas the rail mortises have the " wedging " made at the back of the stiles, the other two mortises must be made with the wedging at the front or face, the reason for which will be apparent later on.

The width rod is shown in Fig. 85 A, and, although this is set out to the full width of the door, as shown, yet the rails (as in Fig. 85 B) are set out to one half only, so that both halves of the door will be exactly the same width.

The setting out of the rails is very simple, owing to the absence of mortises ; but in marking off the various distances due allowance must be made for the bead which parts the two middle stiles, which should be made wider by $\frac{5}{8}$ in. (this being the proper

C   B

FIG. 84.—HEIGHT ROD AND STILES MARKED OUT.

width of bead to use), so that all the stiles will appear the same width on the finished door.

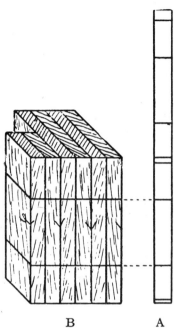

B A

FIG. 85.—WIDTH ROD AND RAILS.

For this reason also the middle stiles must be gauged to a parallel width, and both edges squared. These stiles can be either tongued together (as in Fig. 86) or rebated (as in Fig. 87). In the former the bead is run on the same stile at each side of the

FIG. 86.—MIDDLE STILES TONGUED TOGETHER.

door, thus making it necessary for this stile only to be of extra width. There is not much to choose between

the two methods ; but the writer prefers the tongue
(Fig. 86), as being somewhat easier to do and as
affording a better hold for the glue in putting together.

The method of putting this door together is rather

FIG. 87.—MIDDLE STILES REBATED.

more complicated than for other doors, and for that
reason it will, perhaps, be as well if we describe
it in full.   We will, therefore, presume that the stiles
are mortised and ploughed for the panels, the two
inner ones also beaded and ploughed for tongues—
or rebated, as preferred—the rails tenoned and

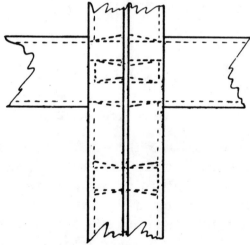

FIG. 88.—WEDGING INNER STILES TOGETHER.

ploughed, and the haunches cut into wedges.   We
shall also require two pieces of hard wood to fit the
mortises A A long enough to reach through the pair
of stiles.

All being ready, and the glue hot, first glue all the rails into the inner stiles only, wedging them tightly ; then cut off the wedges and tenons, so that the stiles will joint closely together, and glueing the tongues into the grooves, and also glueing the joint well; cramp up together, and insert the two pieces of hard wood mentioned above in the mortises made for them (glueing them well, of course), and wedge up on the inside of the stiles (see dotted lines in Fig. 88).

It is as well to allow the door to stand a few hours

FIG. 89.—MIDDLE STILE, SLOT MORTISED.

at this stage, if possible, after which the wedges can be cut off to the bottom of the panel grooves, the panels inserted in position, and the outer stiles put on and wedged in the usual way. The reason for making the mortises A with the wedging on the inside is now apparent, and one more necessary precaution must be mentioned ; this is, to make these mortises true to the marks and the pieces which are inserted in them a tight fit in width, otherwise the rails will not line with each other in the two halves of the door, which effectually spoils the appearance.

As far as finishing the door—that is, cleaning off, moulding, etc., this is the same as for those already described, and need not be repeated.

Although the above method is, we believe, the standard one of making these doors yet the alternative ways may well be shown. The principal alteration consists in making the middle stile in one piece instead of two, and the top and bottom rails the same. When made by this method, the middle

B

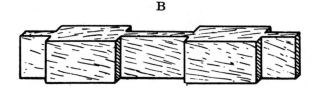

FIG. 90.—ALTERNATIVE METHOD OF TENONING TOP AND BOTTOM RAILS.

stile is slot-mortised, as Fig. 89, the top and bottom rails being tenoned as at B (Fig. 90); the one will then slip into the other, and can be fixed with glue and pins.

A section of such a door, through one rail, is given in Fig. 91, the beads in the middle stile being worked with a centre beading plane.

The great fault of a door put together by this latter method is the tendency of the ends of the middle stile to open, there being no solid wood and nothing to hold them together. To obviate this, they are sometimes shoulder tongued, as in Fig. 92, or

dovetailed, as in Fig. 93.   Either of these methods
answers the purpose ; but they require careful work,
and of the two the former is to be preferred, as the
straight line of the stiles is preserved.   The middle

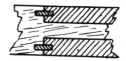

FIG. 91.—SECTION OF ALTER-
NATIVE CENTRE STILE.

FIG. 92.—MIDDLE STILE
SHOULDER TONGUED.

rails are fixed into the middle stiles by "fox wedging."
Should no centre beading plane be available, the
beads up the centre can be inserted in a groove
made for the purpose, as in Fig. 94, or, if preferred,
a V can be run instead, or any other moulding of
suitable section.

FIG. 93.—MIDDLE STILE
SHOULDER DOVETAILED.

FIG. 94.—INSERTED
BEADS.

The materials of which these doors are made should
be thoroughly dry and seasoned, or the centre joint
will come apart, owing to the stiles shrinking, but not
the tenons.

CHAPTER VIII

SELF-MOULDED DOORS

" SELF," or, as they are sometimes called, " solid " moulded doors, are those which have the moulding worked on the stiles, rails, and muntins, instead of framing these up square and " planting " or " inlaying " the moulding round the panels. These doors, if made properly, have a much neater appearance than the others; but require far more careful work in the making, which probably accounts for the scarcity of this style. If, however, any of our readers wish for anything which is not common, and which looks neat, in their houses, let them try self-moulded doors, and we can promise them that they will not be disappointed with the result.

Fig. 95 shows a finished door of the style we are about to describe, and when it is taken into consideration that—if made as it ought to be—the mouldings on the framing must intersect properly at all angles, it will be understood that not only must the stuff be faced up correctly, but it must also be gauged accurately to a thickness, and the middle rail as well as the two muntins must also be gauged to a width.

The size of the door, as shown, is 6 ft. 6 ins. high by 2 ft. 6 ins. wide ; the bottom and middle rails 9 ins. wide, and the stiles, muntins and top rail, $4\frac{1}{2}$ ins. wide.

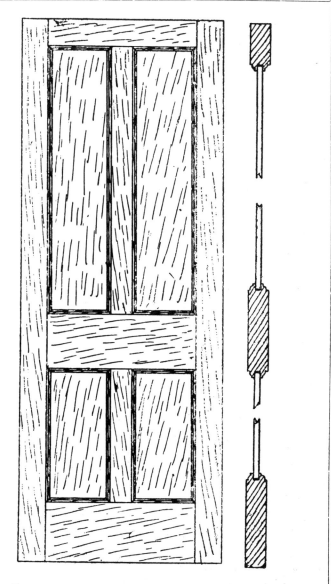

FIG. 95.—SELF-MOULDED DOOR WITH SECTION.

In the vertical section the rails are shown to a larger scale, to show up the mouldings better.

The height rod and the stiles set out from it are shown in Fig. 96. To simplify matters, we have in the example shown the moulding as being $\frac{1}{2}$ in. wide only, so that the lines for depth of grooves (that is the mortise lines) are the same as the moulding lines. Thus the lines A give full height of finished door, B are mortises, and C haunchings. The various distances are marked on the drawing ; the haunchings, however, are only approximately correct, as they must be allowed to come as they will, according to the width the rails are gauged to.

The marks D must be made very exactly to the actual width of the rails, and squared across the edges of the stiles with a cut mark, as these will be the guides for mitreing the moulding later on.

The muntins are shown set out from the rod at E and here will be seen the difference between this and the preceding examples, as formerly the shoulders of the muntins were cut to the marks corresponding to D in Fig. 96. In this case, however, the shoulders have to be made to the mortise lines, as shown by dotted lines from the rod to E.

The width rod, and the three rails as set out from it, are shown in Fig. 97. The mortises for muntins are shown at E, and the mark F must be exact to the actual width of the muntins as guides for mitreing. This also applies to the marks G, which, in the case of an ordinary door, would be the shoulder lines. Here, however, the shoulder lines must be the width of the moulding longer, as at H.

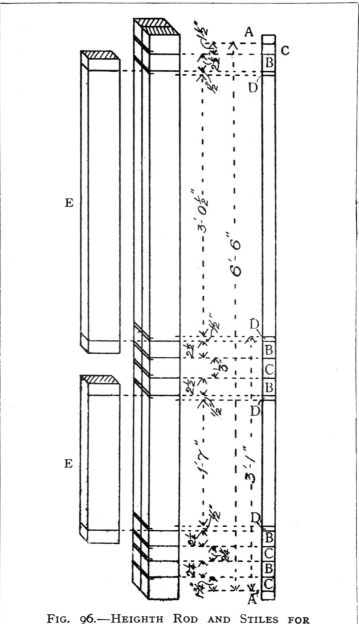

FIG. 96.—HEIGHTH ROD AND STILES FOR
SELF-MOULDED DOOR.

The method of mortising, tenoning, and ploughing the various parts of the door is exactly the same as described before. We can, therefore, consider these operations as done, and pass on to the next, that is the moulding, various patterns of which are shown in Fig. 98.

Having chosen the pattern of moulding required (which, however, must be done before the door is set

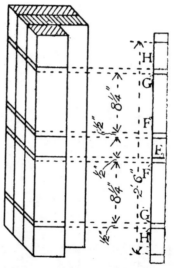

Fig. 97.—Setting-out the Rails.

out), the stiles and top and bottom rails must be moulded on two corners only, while the middle rail and muntins must be done on all four corners, and *then* the shoulders can be cut—not before; after which comes the most particular part of the job, that is, mitreing the mouldings where they intersect. This is done with a sharp chisel, using a template as a guide, and starting the cut at the marks D and G on the

stiles and muntins and the rails respectively. **Fig.** 99
shows the mitres cut on the top rail, and the **stile**
to which the top rail fits.

The rails to which the muntins come, and the
stiles where the middle rail comes, are mitred at
each end of the mortises, the square part of the
moulding between being cut entirely away, and
unless these are cut carefully, they will not fit, and
there is no way of making them do so after. It
is, therefore, better to cut away too little than

A   B   C   D

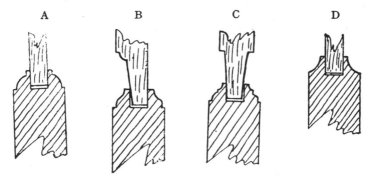

FIG. 98.—VARIOUS PATTERNS OF MOULDING.

too much, easing the mitres slightly afterwards if
required.

In such doors as we are now describing, the grooves
at the ends of the stiles must be made deeper to
receive the haunching on the rail, as shown at I,
Fig. 99, as the ordinary grooves are cut away in
making the mitres.

As stated above, the present door is shown with the
mouldings the same depth as the plough groove, to
prevent confusion : this, however, is not often the
case in practice, as the mouldings may be much

wider, when the rails require setting out so much
longer in the shoulders. They may also be moulded
with a narrow moulding at one side and a wider one

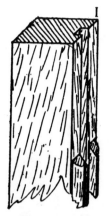

FIG. 99.—TOP RAIL AND STILE, WITH MITRES CUT.

at the other, as shown in Fig. 100; in which
case the shoulders at one side must be longer than
at the other, as in Fig. 101.

If possible, when a door is moulded with a wide
moulding at one side only, the panel should be kept
further from that side, as shown by the groove in
A, Fig. 100.

FIG. 100.—ALTERNATIVE MOULDINGS, WITH ONE
SIDE WIDER.

The panels for self-moulded doors should be thick-
nessed throughout (as A and D Fig. 98), not bevelled
as usual in common doors; or if a better appearance

is desired, they may be raised on one or both sides, as Fig. 98 C, or raised and moulded as Fig. 98 B.

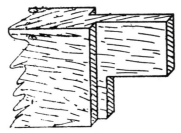

FIG. 101.— RAIL, WITH ONE SHOULDER LONGER THAN THE OTHER.

CHAPTER IX

Door Frames

A HANDBOOK on doors would hardly be complete without some reference to door frames, and in this chapter we propose to give a short description of the various kinds of frames in general use, and to show how to set out and make them.

Fig. 102 is the elevation of an ordinary frame, consisting of two posts or jambs, sill and head : a rebate is formed in the posts and head, to correspond with the thickness of the door, and the other edge is usually chamfered or beaded in some way, as shown in Figs. 103 to 105. The standard size for the scantlings used for door frames is $4\frac{1}{2}$ ins. by 3 ins., although in special cases these are varied as circumstances demand. The rebate should always be made so that the widest way of the stuff takes the thrust of the door, as shown in the above-mentioned drawings. Fig. 106 shows the rebate made the opposite way, as usual in some parts of the country, but this is a very faulty style, the posts yielding every time the door is slammed.

In facing up the timber, the face (or rebate) edge, should be the outside of the tree as it was grown : this can be ascertained by the grain at the end, the correct form being as in Fig. 107, incorrect as Fig. 108. Attention to this apparently unimportant matter makes all the difference to the springing of the posts,

as, if formed as in Fig. 107, the wall keeps them straight
and the door will not require easing; whereas if made
as Fig. 108, the posts will spring into the doorway,
and the door will require frequent easing to make it
work freely.

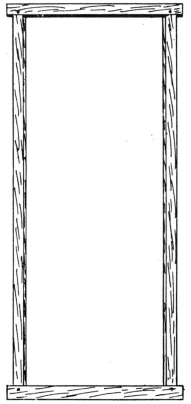

FIG. 102.—ORDINARY DOOR FRAME.

Fig. 109 shows the setting out of the posts: at the
sill end the two shoulders are straight across as on
the right; but at the head the shoulders at the face side
must be ½ in. longer, to fit up into the rebate, as at A,

this shoulder being made to the height of the door.
The above setting out applies to the section of frame
as Fig. 103, where the chamfers are made on the posts

FIG. 103.   FIG. 104.   FIG. 105.

SECTIONS OF DOOR-FRAMING.

only, and the head left square, as in Fig. 110, or to any
other section where the ornamentation is on the posts
only. If the section as Fig. 104 is used, the bead is

FIG. 106.—FAULTY METHOD OF FORMING REBATE.

usually taken round the head, as in Fig. 111, and then
both shoulders will be of an equal length, the bead
being mitred at the intersection.

FIG. 107.   FIG. 108.

SHOWING HOW THE GRAIN SHOULD RUN IN THE POSTS.

This also applies to Fig. 105, where an extra length
must be allowed beyond the height of the door, to

allow for the bead on the edge of the rebate; both this and the large chamfer running round the head, as in Fig. 112. This latter should not be mitred at the angles, but the posts should be scribed to fit the

FIG. 109.—SETTING-OUT DOOR POSTS.

head, as in section Fig. 113. Should it be preferred to stop the chamfers, as Fig. 114, the first setting out will be the correct one.

The setting out of the head and sill is shown in Fig. 115. The mortise lines are not affected in any way by the section of the frame, provided that the tenons are kept to the square portion,

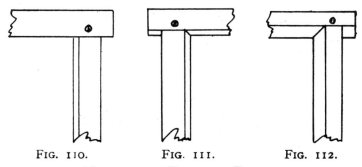

FIG. 110.　　　　FIG. 111.　　　　FIG. 112.

METHODS OF FINISHING FRAMES.

the rebate coming to one side, as in the section (dotted lines), Figs. 103 to 105. Sufficient length must be left on the head and sill to allow them to project at least 1½ ins. beyond the jambs, when

the frame is together, and slot mortises should always
be used. The projecting horns of the head and
sill are cut as Fig. 116, A or B, according to the
thickness of the wall they stand in, and also

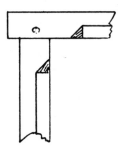

FIG. 113.—SECTION OF   FIG. 114.—STOP CHAMFERS
    SCRIBED HEAD.   ON FRAME.

according to the position they occupy in the wall ;
the bricks, being cut to fit the horns, hold the
frame tightly.

Fig. 117 shows the upper end of a door jamb after
the tenon is cut, section as Fig. 103. In some parts of
the country the sills of outside door frames—that is ,
the frames which are fixed in the outer walls of house
or building of any kind—are made wider than the
jambs, and are bevelled, as Fig. 118, the bevel starting

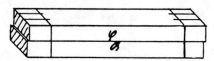

FIG. 115.—SETTING-OUT THE HEAD AND SILL.

at the rebate line. This is a very good idea, the wet
having a better chance of getting away ; but in these
days of cheapness it is too often considered that the
extra work of bevelling the sill and cutting the

shoulders to fit takes too long ; it is, however, the proper thing to do.

Inside doors are usually hung in " jamb linings," instead of door frames, these being fixed in the

A B

FIG. 116.—METHODS OF CUTTING HEAD AND SILL TO HOLD IN BRICKWORK.

walls after the house is built. Too often they are made from thin stuff only, but they should not be less than 2 ins. thick ; in width they should be sufficient to project each side of the wall and finish level with the plaster. No sill is used with jamb linings, and the head is trenched to take the jambs as Fig. 119, the jamb being cut to fit as Fig. 120.

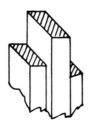

FIG. 117.—UPPER END OF JAMB, SHOWING TENON.

FIG. 118.—BEVELLED SILL.

An easier way of forming the linings is to fix them solid and nail on a thin piece to form the rebate, as in Fig. 121. One advantage of this style is, the rebate can be fixed after the door is hung : thus, if the latter is crooked or twists, it can be rectified to a certain extent.

In good houses, where the walls are thick, the jamb

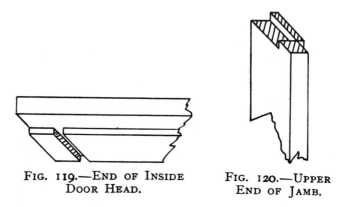

FIG. 119.—END OF INSIDE DOOR HEAD.

FIG. 120.—UPPER END OF JAMB.

linings are panelled, as in Fig. 122, or too often they are formed as Fig. 121, but with a narrow solid piece at each side of the opening, the thin board forming the rebate covering the intervening space. In all cases when fixing linings, it is best to fix blocks be-

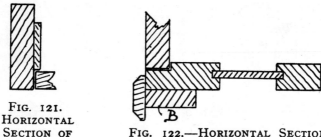

FIG. 121. HORIZONTAL SECTION OF ORDINARY JAMB.

FIG. 122.—HORIZONTAL SECTION OF PANELLED JAMB.

hind at the spot where the hinges will come, as B, Fig. 122, to give the screws better hold.

The linings are fixed to plugs driven into the wall,

unless "grounds" are fixed to take them, which is not often the case, though it always should be done. Wood bricks for fixing are convenient, but are not to be depended on, being apt to work loose.

The most convenient method of making rebates in

FIG. 123.—METHOD OF FORMING REBATES IN JAMBS AND HEADS.

the jambs and heads is shown in A and B, Fig. 123: the groove is ploughed first to the required depth, as A, and the wood roughly removed with the chisel as B, the rebate then finished down to the gauge mark with badger or rebate plane.

CHAPTER X

FITTING AND HANGING DOORS

THE fitting and hanging (or hingeing) of doors in a proper manner, is quite as important as the making, therefore we include the present chapter in this handbook, with the idea that it would not be complete otherwise.

To fit a panel door of any description, first take the exact width of the opening and transfer to the door, taking a piece off each stile if necessary, so that these will appear of equal width. If the door simply requires planing, which is as it should be, or if wider, after sawing off the waste at each side, plane the left-hand stile and fit it to the corresponding post, then do likewise with the other, making the door so that when close up to one side there is a space of a sixteenth of an inch parallel at the other.

The door must now be placed in position, close up to one post, as in Fig. 124, and scribed along the bottom with compasses. Whether the projecting stiles only are cut off, or a certain portion of the bottom rail as well, depends upon the height of the door compared with the opening. If the one is much higher than the other, a good portion of the waste should be removed from the bottom rail, leaving the top rail the same width as the stiles. This, of course, must be ascertained by actual measurement before scribing. Having scribed and cut off the bottom of the door, stand it up again, and mark the height required on the stiles, and in cutting off at the top, allow for the same play here as at each side and slightly more at the bottom.

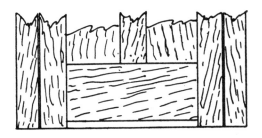

FIG. 124.—DOOR IN POSITION FOR SCRIBING.

In planing the edges of the door, that on the hanging side may be planed exactly square; but it is best to plane the other edge slightly under, as at A, Fig. 125, thus giving the door more clearance as it opens: especially does this apply to thick doors—in fact, in many cases the rebates are bevelled if the doors are thicker than one and a half inches.

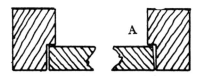

FIG. 125.—SECTION SHOWING HOW TO FIT THE DOOR.

The fitting of ledge doors is the same as described above, except that so much trouble need not be taken, there being no stiles to keep equal in width.

For outside doors the play at sides and especially

at the bottom must be greater than for inside, otherwise they will be liable to stick and require easing ;
while in many cases more play must be allowed at
the bottom of room doors, to allow these to open
over carpet or linoleum : of this, more later on.

A　　　　　　　　　　　　　B

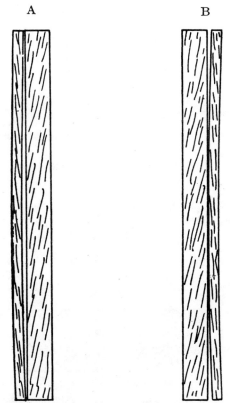

FIG. 126.—RIGHT AND WRONG WAYS OF PLACING A DOOR.

If the doors are alike both sides, as in ordinary
room doors, the hollow side (if the door is not flat, as
is sometimes the case) must be fitted towards the
rebates, as in Fig. 126 A—the fastening will then keep

the door tight ; but if the round side is put to the
rebates, as Fig. 126 B, there will always be a space at

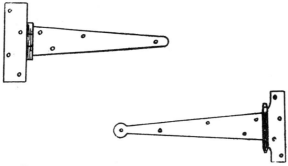

FIG. 127.—CROSS-GARNETT OR T-HINGES.

top and bottom, and the door will also rub the post
in the middle, at the hinge side, as it opens.

For ledge doors the usual hinges are the " cross

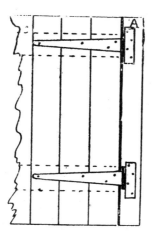

FIG. 128.—SHOWING HOW HINGES SHOULD BE PUT ON.

garnett " or " tee " hinges, examples of which are
given in Fig. 127. The fixing of these is very

simple : the door is stood up in position, blocking it so that it has the correct play all round, and the hinges screwed on as in Fig. 128. The top

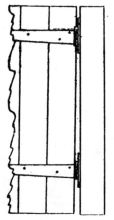

FIG. 129.—EFFECT OF PLACING HINGE BACK ON POST.

hinge should have the knuckle immediately over the joint, but the bottom should be placed back further on to the post as shown. This has the effect

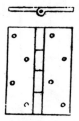

FIG. 130.—FRONT AND END OF BUTT HINGE.

of throwing the front of the door up as it opens, as shown in Fig. 129.

Panel doors are invariably hung with "butt hinges,"

a front and end view of which we show in Fig. 130, and these may be fixed by letting the whole thickness into the door, as Fig. 131 A; by letting half into the door and half into the post, as Fig. 131, B, or

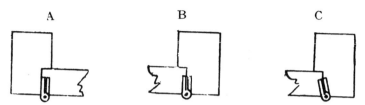

FIG. 131.—WAYS OF FITTING " BUTTS "

by letting them in on the skew, as Fig. 131 C. The first is the jerry builder's method, being done quickly ; the second is the joiner's method, and the correct one for all purposes as regards house doors; while the third is usually adopted by cabinet makers, and is correct for furniture, but more difficult to do properly. The " butts " should be let into the

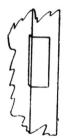

FIG. 132.—SPACE FOR HINGE MARKED OUT.

door first, the correct positions being 6 ins. from the top and 10 ins. from the bottom of the door. The distance on the edge from the face should be slightly less than the width of the butt to the centre of the pin on which it turns, and the depth of the recess should be the thickness of one leaf of the butt. The

A   B

FIG. 133.—EFFECT OF PLACING HINGE TOO FAR IN, AND NOT FAR ENOUGH.

length of the recess should be marked by laying on the butt itself, each one in the position it will fill, as they vary in size slightly.

The recess as marked is shown in Fig. 132, while Fig. 133 A and B show the effect of letting the butt

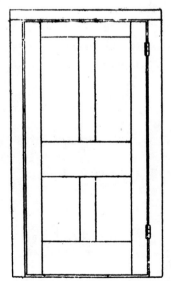

FIG. 134.—EVEN SPACE ALL ROUND DOOR.

in too far on the edge, and not far enough respectively, the one causing the door to scrape the frame as it opens,

and the other leaving an ugly gap between when the
door is open. After letting the butts into the door,
and screwing them tightly, the door should be placed,
in position, blocking it so that it has its proper play
all round, as in Fig. 134. Then with the butts open,

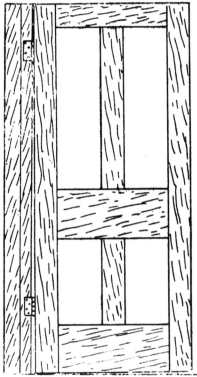

Fig. 135.—Lower Butt Projecting to Make Door Rise.

mark on the frame at the bottom and top of each
for the height, and down by the knuckle for the
depth of the recess. The door can then be removed,
the height marks squared across, and the gauge used
for the width. On cutting the wood out to the marks,

the door may be fixed temporarily with one screw in each butt, and if found to be correct (as it should be) the remaining screws can be inserted, while, if not correct, alteration must be made accordingly.

In the above description we are assuming that the door and frame are both made true—that the door is

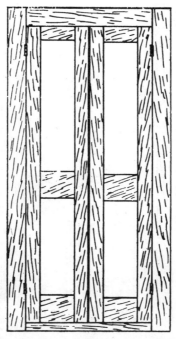

FIG. 136.—DOORS WITH RAILS OUT OF LINE.

of parallel thickness, and the rebate slightly deeper to give the necessary play; but in many cases we regret to say that the frame is rebated without any regard to the thickness of the door, and if so, the door may either bind on the rebate, if the latter is not deep enough, or may not fit close enough to it, if too deep.

To get over this difficulty, the gauging for the width of the recess should be done from the edge of the rebate, and the inside of the door respectively, taking great care that the hinges are not let in far enough to make the door bind, as in A Fig. 133.

Doors may be made to rise as they open by using

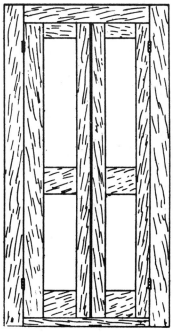

FIG. 137.—DOORS WITH UNEVEN STILES.

rising butts, but these are clumsy in appearance: the only difficulty in fixing is to take special care to get them fitted correctly, and also to get them the right hand for the door, or they will throw the door down instead of up.

Instead of using rising butts, the door may be made to rise in front as it opens, by allowing the bottom butt to project more than the top one, as in Fig. 135. This means different gauging for each butt, but it often has to be done, the floors in many cases being low at the doorway, owing to the weight of the walls causing the joists to settle slightly.

Spring butts, both double and single, are fixed in exactly the same way, and also all other kinds of hinges, the principle being the same throughout.

One word as to fitting of folding doors : care should be taken to keep the outside stiles on each door the same width, even if the middle stiles are not exactly the same. Also take care to keep the rails in each pair of doors level, or the appearance is spoiled. Fig. 136 shows a pair of doors correct in respect to the former point, but incorrect as to the latter ; while Fig. 137 is the reverse—the rails are right, but the stiles are uneven. A little care in fitting will make both right, and there is no excuse for neglecting it.

WINDOW-MAKING

For Carpenters and Joiners

SHOWING HOW TO SET OUT AND CONSTRUCT
WINDOW SASHES AND FRAMES

CONTENTS

WINDOW-MAKING

CHAPTER I

CASEMENT WINDOW FRAMES

OF the making of windows there is no end, and, while it is obvious that we cannot in this little handbook deal with all and every kind, we propose to deal with those in common use, commencing with the most simple, and following up gradually towards the more elaborate.

Some of those shown will be recognised by all, as they are in general use throughout the length and breadth of the land ; but others may be quite strange to some of our readers, through being localised to a great extent.

In reference to these latter, it is an open question if they could not be introduced with advantage in districts where they are unknown. As an example worthy of wider extension, we might mention the sliding sashes described in Chapter V.

Casement windows are those in which the sashes which open are hinged, either at the sides or at the top, opening either outwards or inwards ; they are the most simple of all windows, and, therefore, we have chosen to treat these first.

The outside elevation of an ordinary casement

frame is shown in Fig. 1, and it consists of the sill A, the head B, the jambs C, and the mullion D. These parts are all, in technical language, termed "solid wrought"—that is, worked out of the solid

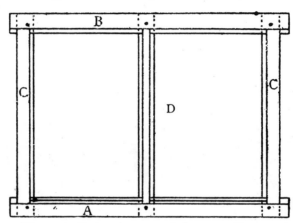

FIG. 1.—ELEVATION OF CASEMENT FRAME.

wood, in contradistinction to the cased frames to be described later on.

The usual dimensions of the scantlings are $4\frac{1}{2}$ ins. wide by 3 ins. thick; but sometimes the sill is wider, so as to project beyond the jambs on the outside.

Fig. 2 is a horizontal section of a casement frame in which the sashes fit in rebates, and are flush with

FIG. 2.—CROSS SECTION OF CASEMENT FRAME.

the outside of the frame; enlarged sections of the sill, jambs, and mullion being given in Figs. 3, 4, and 5, respectively—the dotted lines in the two latter showing position of mortise and tenon.

Fig. 6 shows a section of a frame in which the rebates are formed by nailing on beads, as E. The sills, jambs, and mullion are also bevelled, as shown in the enlarged sections (Figs. 7, 8, and 9); and the sashes stand in from the front, as shown

FIG. 3.—SECTION OF SILL (FIG 2). FIG. 4.—SECTION OF JAMB (FIG. 2). FIG. 5.—SECTION OF MULLION (FIG. 2).

by dotted lines in Fig. 6. The head of this frame is not bevelled, but is as Fig. 10.

In Fig. 11 we have a section of a better class of casement frame, in which the inside of the jambs, mullion, and head are moulded, and the outside chamfered, as in sections (Figs. 12 and 13), the former representing both jamb and head. The sill is also double-sunk, as in Fig. 14, the additional water bar F being nailed on after the frame is made.

In this latter frame, the sashes finish level with the edge of the outside chamfer, as dotted lines

FIG. 6.—CROSS SECTION OF REBATE CASEMENT FRAME.

in Fig. 11, and to the second sinking of the sill G (Fig. 14). The sill in this case is a projecting one, being 1½ ins. wider than the other framing, which is supposed to be 4½ ins. by 4 ins. ; thus the sill is 6 ins. by 4 ins.

All sills should be of oak, and all other parts of yellow deal; but in many cases, for cheap work, the sills are also made of deal.

Having said so much by way of introduction, we can now proceed to set out the frame shown

FIG. 7.—SECTION OF SILL (FIG. 6).

FIG. 8.—SECTION OF JAMB (FIG. 6).

in section in Fig. 2, taking for granted that all the materials are faced up correctly in the regulation manner.

The width-rod (H H) is shown at the right-hand side of Fig. 15, set out as required. The marks H show full width of the frame outside; from these, inwards, set off the thickness of jambs to marks I, and midway between, set out the thickness of the mullion K. Each of these thicknesses must be

FIG. 9.—SECTION OF MULLION (FIG. 6).

FIG. 10.—SECTION OF HEAD (FIG. 6).

ascertained by measuring the parts concerned, not by marking off 3 ins. because 3-in. stuff is being used.

To set out the sill and head, lay them face to face, as in Fig. 15, transfer the lines I and K to them, as shown by the dotted lines, and square across on both the face and inner sides. The end mortises being slotted, the marks H are not needed on the framing at all.

The mortise gauge must be set so that a space

FIG. 11.—CROSS SECTION OF MOULDED CASEMENT FRAME.

is left on the outside (L) equal to the thickness of the sashes to be used, and the remaining width can then be divided equally for mortise and shoulder. The former is shown by the shaded portion in Fig. 15.

FIG. 12.—SECTION OF
JAMB AND HEAD (FIG. 11).

FIG. 13.—SECTION OF
MULLION (FIG. 11).

The height-rod (M M) is shown set out in Fig. 16, the marks M being the full height of the frame outside; from these set off, inwards, the thickness of sill and head, thus obtaining the marks N. At

FIG. 14.—SECTION OF SILL (FIG. 11).

the top end set off outwards from N ½ in. for the rebate, and make the mark O; and at the sill end set off outwards from N 1 in. to the mark P (½ in.

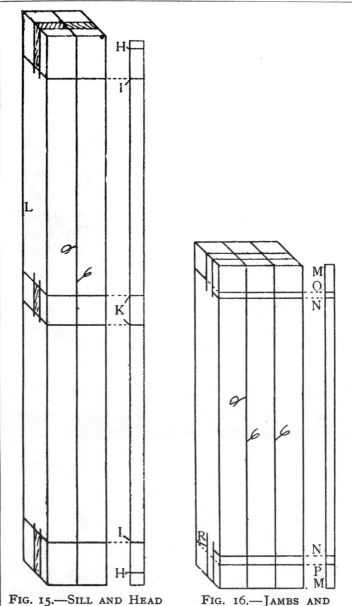

FIG. 15.—SILL AND HEAD
SET OUT FROM WIDTH
ROD (FIGS. 1 AND 2).

FIG. 16.—JAMBS AND
MULLION SET OUT FROM
HEIGHT ROD.

for the rebate, and another ½ in. for the bevel of the sill, Fig. 3).

Now lay the jambs and mullion on the bench in the following order : First, one jamb, face upwards and outwards ; then the mullion, facing the same way ; then the other jamb, face downwards and outwards, as in Fig. 16.

The lines N, O, P must be transferred to the framing from the rod, as leading lines, and squared

FIG. 17.—JAMB WITH SHOULDERS CUT (FIG. 6).

over on the face, as shown ; N being the shoulder line at both head and sill on the inside, but O is the shoulder at the head, and P at the sill on the outside. The latter must be cut on the bevel, as at R, bringing it ½ in. longer than N at the outside of the tenon.

The frame in Fig. 6 is set out in exactly the same way as the above, but all the mortises must be marked with a bevel instead of square, and the shoulders as well on the outside ; the bevelled lines

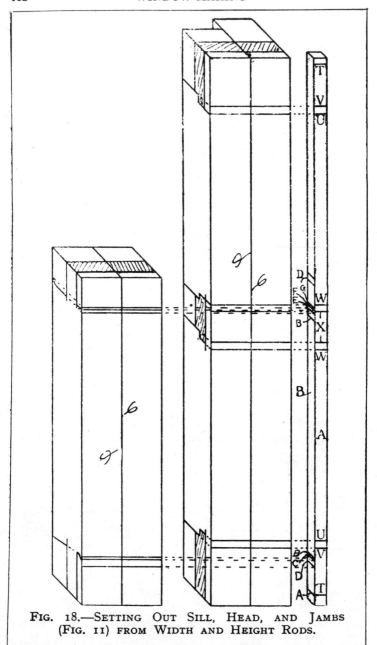

FIG. 18.—SETTING OUT SILL, HEAD, AND JAMBS
(FIG. 11) FROM WIDTH AND HEIGHT RODS.

in both cases commencing at the point where the inner gauge line cuts the inside shoulder line, thus the jambs with shoulders cut will be as Fig. 17, the bevel to fit the sill S being ranged to come $\frac{1}{2}$ in. longer than the inside shoulder, at the inside of the tenon, instead of outside.

The setting out of the frame in Fig. 11 is more complicated, on account of the moulding on the inside and the chamfer on the outside, as well as the mortise coming partly in the rebate.

The width-rod is shown in Fig. 18 (A). The marks T show the width of the frame outside, and from these set off inwards the thickness of the jambs, making the marks U, and at $\frac{5}{8}$ in. outwards from these make marks V. Mid-way between U and V make the marks W the thickness of mullion between, and X $\frac{5}{8}$ in. inwards from W.

Transfer the marks U, V, W, and X to the sill and head, as in Fig. 18, and square over as shown. Set the mortise gauge so that it gives $1\frac{1}{2}$-in. mortise, one side of which comes to the square of the moulding to be worked on it, as dotted lines in Fig. 13 ; also set a marking gauge to the edge of the rebate Y (Fig. 13), and run this on the sill and head, thus giving the set off in the mortises, as shown by the shaded portions in Fig. 18.

The height-rod of this frame is shown in Fig. 18 (B), set out on the side of A. The marks A are the full height of the frame ; from these inwards set off the thickness of the sill and head, thus giving B ; then at the bottom end for the sill set off $\frac{1}{4}$ in. for C, and 1 in. for D.

At the head end, set off outwards from B ⅝ in.
to E, 1 in. to F, and 1¼ ins. to G.   The marks B,
C, and D must be transferred to the jamb and mullion
at the sill end, and E, F, and G at the head end,
as in Fig. 18 (in which jambs appear at the left),
and squared across, as shown.   The marks C and D
form the inside and outside shoulders respectively,
at the sill end : the former being cut to an angle
of 45° to fit the small chamfer on the sill on the

FIG. 19.—JAMB WITH SHOULDERS CUT (FIG. 11).

inside, and the latter being cut to the bevel to fit
the slope of the sill on the outside, as in Fig. 19 ;
the line B gives the part to be cut away at H.

At the head end, the shoulders proper are the
marks F and G on the inside and outside respectively, E being the straight cut to fit the rebate I
(Fig. 19) ; the shoulder being cut to an angle of
45° to fit the outside chamfer, as at K.

On the inside the shoulder is cut square, being

afterwards scribed to fit the moulding, as at C. As this scribing will be fully described, and the method illustrated, when we come to the sashes, we can pass it over at present.

The setting out finished, all mortises and tenons should be sawn in—but not the shoulders cut—after which all mouldings, rebates, and chamfers must be worked; then shoulders cut, pin holes bored, and all parts fitted together, and when brought to a proper fit, the frame can be pinned up and cleaned off.

All such frames as these should be fixed together by draw-boring—wedges are quite useless—and all joints must be made to fit without using force. If the latter has to be applied to bring the parts together, it is a sign of bad workmanship; it should not be necessary to use the cramps at all, the pins being quite capable of bringing the joints up if made properly.

CHAPTER II

Casement Sashes

We have now to make the sashes for the frames which were described in Chap. I, and the first thing to do is to take the correct measurements for same, which is best done by cutting a rod to just fit in the rebates, for both height and width, but it will not do to cut it to fit close to the rebates, or the sashes will come too short in height, on account of the bevelled sill ; and in frames where the jambs and muntins are also bevelled, as Fig. 6 (Chap. I), they would also come too narrow. It therefore follows that the dimensions for the sashes must be taken at the thickness of the sashes from the rebate, both in height and width.

The elevation and section of one sash is shown in Fig. 20, and the better to illustrate the methods of making, we have shown it with both upright and cross bars. The technical terms for the various parts are as follows : A stiles, B bottom rail, C top rail, D upright bar, E cross bar.

The stiles and top rails are usually the same size, 2 ins. wide by $1\frac{1}{2}$ ins. thick, or $2\frac{1}{4}$ ins. by $1\frac{3}{4}$ ins. respectively, accordingly to the thickness specified. The bottom rail is usually $3\frac{1}{2}$ ins. and 4 ins. for the two thicknesses of sashes mentioned. The bars should be $\frac{3}{4}$ in. thick.

The sections of the stiles and top rails are shown

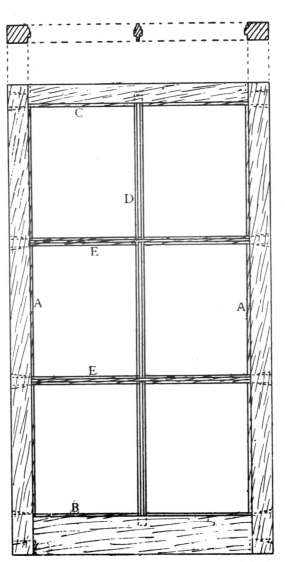

Fig. 20.—Elevation and Section of Casement
Sash.

in Fig. 21, of the bottom rail in Fig. 22, and of the
bars in Fig. 23 (at F). It will be noticed that the
rebates in the whole of these sections are worked

FIG. 21.—SECTION OF STILE
AND TOP RAIL.

FIG. 22.—SECTION OF
BOTTOM RAIL.

down exactly the same distance as the mouldings,
thus bringing the shoulders both the same length.
The bars are sometimes worked to the section shown
in Fig. 24, but this only makes more work, without

FIG. 23.—SECTION OF
BAR.

FIG. 24.—FAULTY SECTION
OF BAR.

any corresponding benefit, and is not to be recommended.

For the sake of illustration, the sash, as shown,

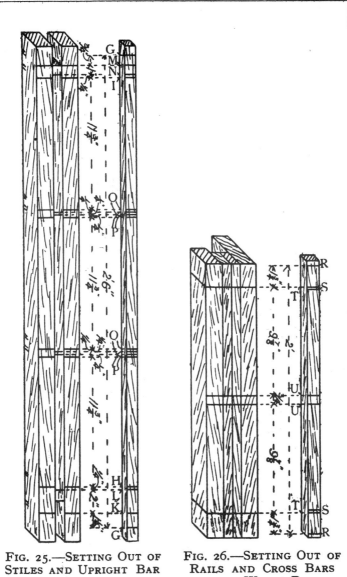

FIG. 25.—SETTING OUT OF
STILES AND UPRIGHT BAR
FROM HEIGHT ROD.

FIG. 26.—SETTING OUT OF
RAILS AND CROSS BARS
FROM WIDTH ROD

is made to scale, being 3½ ft. high by 2 ft. wide, and the height-rod is shown set out to this size in Fig. 25 (G G). First make the marks G, at 3½ ft. apart, showing the required height of the sash, then from one of these measure off the width of the bottom rail, and make the mark H, also the width of the top rail from the other mark G, thus getting the mark I. From H and I measure off (towards the end of the rod in each case) 2¼ ins., and 1¼ ins. respectively for length of mortises, making the marks K and M; and also from H and I, in the same direction, measure off the distance which the moulding plane works down to (which must be ascertained by working it on a waste piece of wood), making the two marks L and N.

Now measure the exact distance between H and I, and, after deducting the thickness of the two cross bars, divide exactly into three parts, and set off one from H and one from I, then the thickness of the bar from each, thus getting the four marks O, when, if the dividing is done equally, there will be found the same distance between the two bars as from the bars to the bottom and top rails.

Now set off the depth of the moulding from the marks O, and make the four marks P, which will finish the setting out, as far as the height-rod is concerned. We can, therefore, follow on with the stuff itself, taking it for granted that it is already faced up and gauged to a thickness.

The stiles and upright bar are shown set out from the rod in Fig. 25. To do this, first lay one stile on the bench, face side up, and face edge towards you; then the bar the same way; and, lastly, the second stile in the same way, but face side down.

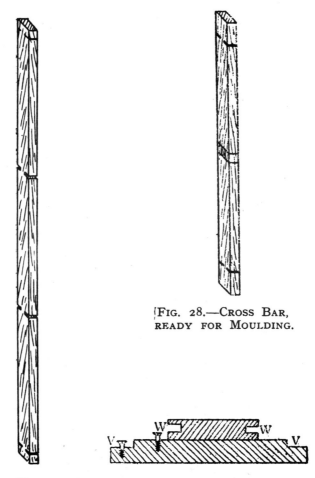

FIG. 28.—CROSS BAR, READY FOR MOULDING.

FIG. 27.—UPRIGHT BAR, READY FOR MOULDING.

FIG. 29.—SECTION OF STICKING BOARD.

Lay the rod on top of the latter stile, so that the marks can be squared down across the whole, those representing the mortises (H, I, K, M, and O) on to the stiles only, and the shoulder marks (L, N, and P) on to the bar only. The whole of these should be made with knife or chisel, not with pencil.

The mortise marks must be squared across at the top and down on the other side, also making

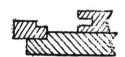

FIG. 31.—BAR IN POSITION FOR MAKING FIRST REBATE.

FIG. 30.—PLAN OF STICKING BOARD.

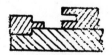

FIG. 32.—BAR REVERSED FOR SECOND REBATE.

additional marks for the wedgings, as shown. All of these may be made with the pencil.

The marks on the bar must be squared across the side and on the edge, using the knife as before.

The width-rod is shown in Fig. 26 (R R), the marks R showing the full width of the sash (2 ft.) ;

from these set off 2 ins. (the width of the stiles), thus getting the marks S, and back from these, the depth of the moulding, as on the stiles, which gives us the shoulder lines T. Midway between make the marks U, for the mortises to take the upright bar.

The rails and cross bars should be laid on the

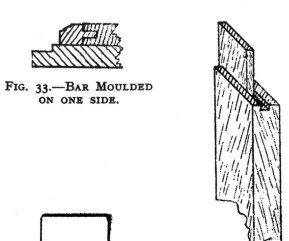

FIG. 33.—BAR MOULDED
ON ONE SIDE.

FIG. 34.—BENCH
KNIFE.

FIG. 35.—RAIL WITH TENON
CUT AND HAUNCHED.

bench in the order shown in Fig. 26, first the bottom rail (face side up), then the two bars, and, lastly, the top rail (face side down). The marks T and U must then be transferred to the whole from the rod, using the chisel throughout.

The shoulder lines T must be squared across on each side of the rails, but not the mortise lines U, as these require stubbing in only. On the bars the shoulder lines T must be squared across on one side, and on to the other edge; but the mortise lines U must be squared across at both sides.

The lines S must be squared down at the back side of the rails only, as guides for cutting out the haunchings.

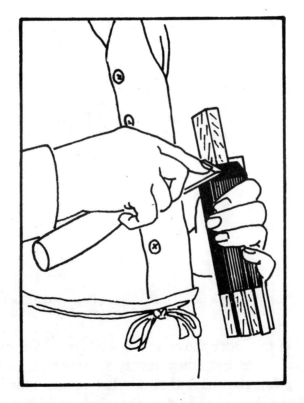

FIG. 36.—MITREING SASH MOULDING FOR SCRIBING.

The mortise gauge should be set so that one line comes to the edge of the moulding, and to suit the width of a chisel, always remembering to leave a good rebate. The proportions shown in sections

(Figs. 21 and 22) are about right, the dotted lines in the former showing the position of the mortise.

The rails must be gauged for tenons and mortises, the bars for mortises only. The latter must be

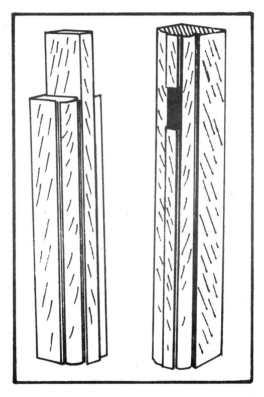

FIG. 37.—RAIL AND STILE BEFORE SCRIBING.

made entirely, and the tenons sawn in before the mouldings and rebates are made, but the shoulders must not be cut on the rails. On the bars, however, this procedure is reversed—the shoulders being cut, but not the tenons. Thus, when the bars have

reached this stage, and are ready for moulding, the
upright one is as Fig. 27, and the cross one as Fig. 28.

The sticking of the rails and stiles will present
no difficulty; the only thing to be careful of is to
make the rebate exactly the same depth as the
square of the moulding, as stated above, which can
easily be regulated by the depth stop of the sash

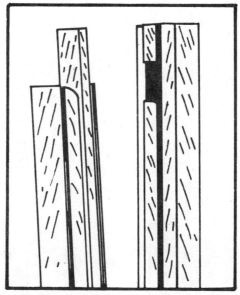

FIG. 38.—RAIL AND STILE AFTER SCRIBING.

fillester. The sticking of the bars will, however,
require a special sticking board to hold them on.
This is shown in section in Fig. 29, and in plan in
Fig. 30, the rebates V and the grooves W being
made to suit bars $1\frac{3}{4}$ ins. by $\frac{7}{8}$ in. on one edge of the
board, and $1\frac{1}{2}$ ins. by $\frac{3}{4}$ in. on the other edge.

The manner of using the sticking board is shown

in Figs. 31, 32, and 33, the bar being shown in position for making the first rebate (Fig. 31), reversed for second rebate (Fig. 32), and for making the first moulding (Fig. 33). To make the second moulding, the bar is simply reversed and placed in the same groove.

The two screws shown in Figs. 29 and 30 act as

FIG. 39.—JOINT PARTLY KNOCKED TOGETHER.

stops to the bars while working the mouldings and rebates, the back end being held tightly on the board with a " bench knife." This is simply a small piece of an ordinary table knife, as Fig. 34, and is driven into the board and bar, so that it is below the surface, and will not injure the planes.

After all parts are stuck, the tenons are formed

on the bars by cutting off the mouldings and tongues with a chisel; the long upright bar must also be sawn apart at the two places where the shoulders are cut, as in Fig. 23. All the shoulders on the rails may be cut, and the tenons haunched, cutting the latter back to the marks S, so that they appear as Fig. 35.

All the mouldings have now to be scribed to fit those to which they come at right angles. This is done by first mitreing them, using a template as a guide, as is demonstrated in Fig. 36, and then

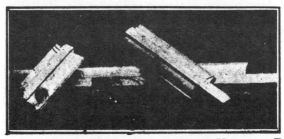

FIG. 40.—CROSS BAR AND PART OF UPRIGHT BAR, SCRIBED.

cutting the surplus away with a scribing or paring gouge. The template must be used on both sides of the bars; but on the rails the gouge only cuts down about ¾ in., the moulding on the stiles being cut away to allow the square shoulder to fit. Thus the rail and stile before scribing are as Fig. 37, and after scribing as Fig. 38; while Fig. 39 shows them partly knocked together.

The cross bar, and two parts of the upright bar, with the scribing done, are shown in Fig. 40, and the three parts put together in Fig. 41.

If more sashes than one are being made, they can all be set out together ; but in this case the bars may be kept separate from stiles and rails, the latter being used to set out the former; the shoulders on the bars may all be cut at once, thus saving considerable time.   The bars should always be kept fully long, to ensure them coming up to a good joint, and they must always be put together the same way they are set out, as if what is set out

FIG. 41.—BARS KNOCKED TOGETHER.

with the bottom end of the stiles is put in at the top, there is great risk of making the cross bars crooked. The same applies to the cross bars : they should never be reversed, or the upright bar will not be straight.

Before cutting up the upright bars they must all be numbered, so that they will come together again in the same order as though they had not been cut.

When ready, all parts should be fitted together, then, if correct, knock off the stiles about half way, glue the tenons and shoulders quickly and liberally,

·cramp up at once, and wedge tightly. Each sash must be tested with the squaring rod diagonally before the wedges are driven home.

The tenons of the rails should all be wedged first, leaving the bars to be done after. When doing the latter, keep an eye on them, or the wedges may force them to one side, making them crooked. This is easily obviated by driving the wedge at one side or the other as required.

CHAPTER III

Cased Sash Frames

THE *cased* sash frame is so called on account of the whole of the frame, with the exception of the sill, being formed of boards only, leaving the inside hollow, so that the weights, on which the sashes are balanced, can slide freely up and down ; thus it is quite different in construction from the solid-framed casement window described in Chap. I.

The specification of the sash frame, as shown in the accompanying drawings, is as follows :—Deal cased frame with oak sunk sill, filled in with $1\frac{3}{4}$-in. sashes, double hung, with best lines and cast-iron weights. Frame to have 3-in. sill, 1-in. pulley stiles, and $\frac{3}{4}$-in. linings, and to be finished with proper dividing tongue and back linings. Parting beads to be 5-16ths in. by $\frac{7}{8}$ in., and staff beads $\frac{5}{8}$ in. by $\frac{7}{8}$ in., and proper water bead to be fixed between sill and staff bead. The sill to be ploughed to receive the window board, also grooved for drip and bed.

In this chapter we deal with the frame only, which is shown complete in elevation in Fig. 42, in vertical section in Fig. 43, and in horizontal section in Fig. 44.

The enlarged section (Fig. 45) enables all the parts to be identified as follows :—A, pulley stile ; B, outside lining ; C, inside lining ; D, parting bead ; E, staff bead ; F, dividing tongue ; and G, back lining. At the top of the frame, the part which corresponds to the pulley stiles is called the head or cap, the two linings being called the outside and inside head linings ; the sill is, of course, understood to be the bottom of the frame.

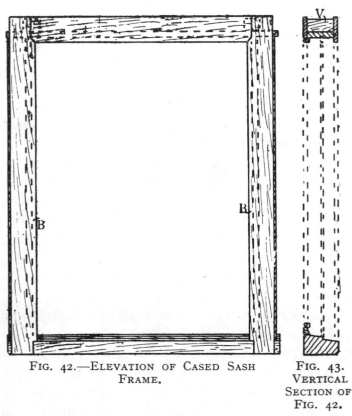

FIG. 42.—ELEVATION OF CASED SASH FRAME.

FIG. 43. VERTICAL SECTION OF FIG. 42.

The dimensions are taken trom the underside of the sill to the underside of the head, for the height, and the width is usually given between the pulley stiles. The exception to this is when the frame has to be made to fit a certain opening, in which case the size given is the extreme outside measurements, or "over all."

The height-rod is shown set out at the right-hand side of Fig. 46, the two marks H being the full height of frame from the bottom of the sill to the under

FIG. 44.—HORIZONTAL SECTION OF FIG. 42.

side of the head; from the bottom H set off 3 ins. for thickness of sill to mark I, and back towards the bottom $1\frac{1}{2}$ ins., the distance the pulley stiles have to enter the sill, which is marked K; also from I set off $4\frac{1}{2}$ ins. and $19\frac{1}{2}$ ins., making L and M, the length of the pocket-pieces.

Now at the top end set off a $\frac{1}{4}$ in. longer than H to N, giving the distance the pulley stiles are tongued

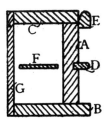

FIG. 45.—ENLARGED SECTION OF ONE SIDE OF SASH FRAME.

into the head and back from H the other way 3 ins., and $5\frac{1}{2}$ ins. giving O, the mortises to receive the pulleys.

The whole of the marks are transferred to the pulley stiles, as shown in the centre of Fig. 46,

and squared across the front, as in Fig. 47. It will
be noticed that in the latter drawing the marks L
and M are not made entirely across, but on the inside
half only; also that the face marks are at the opposite edge; this means that the face edges should

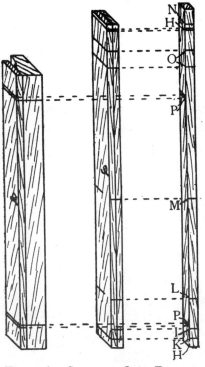

FIG. 46.—SETTING OUT PULLEY,   FIG. 47.—PULLEY
STILES, HEAD, AND SILL FROM   STILES SET OUT
HEIGHT AND WIDTH ROD.   ON FACE.

always be at the outside, whereas the pocket-pieces
are, or should be, on the inside. It will also be
seen that the plough grooves in which the parting
beads have to fit are nearer to the face edges than
to the others, instead of being in the middle; the

reason for this can be seen by a glance at Fig. 45, the staff bead E requiring a ¼ in. of the pulley stile on the inside of the frame, whereas the whole width is available for the sash on the outside.

As regards the width of the frame, very little

FIG. 48.—SILL SET OUT
FOR NOTCHING.

FIG. 49.—SILL WITH
NOTCHES CUT.

setting out is required, as shown on the left side of the rod in Fig. 46, simply the two marks P, and the two others a ¼ in. longer, giving the width of trenches to take the tongue on the top ends of the pulley stiles.

The marks are transferred to head and sill, as shown at the left-hand side of Fig. 46, and all that is required to finish the head is to make the two trenches to the depth of a ¼ in., when it is ready for putting together.

FIG. 50.—SILL WITH RECESSES
FOR LININGS CUT.

FIG. 51.—SILL WITH
BEDDING AND WINDOW
GROOVES MADE.

The sill, however, requires considerably more manipulation : first the marks P must be squared across the top side, and down across the face edge ; then the gauge marks for the depth of the trenches made at 1½ ins. from the top of the sill on the inside, but gauging them from the bottom on both the inside and outside. Next gauge on both top and bottom, inside and outside, ⅝ in. the thickness of the linings, and, lastly, mark across for the wedging, which should be dovetailed to prevent the wedges drawing out in driving.

The sill will now be as Fig. 48, and when the dovetailed trenches are cut it should be as Fig. 49, while at the next stage, when the lining recesses

FIG. 52.—SECTION OF
POCKET-PIECE.

FIG. 53.—METHOD OF
CUTTING POCKET-PIECES
AT BACK.

are cut out, it will be as Fig. 50. The sill is now finished except the grooving for the window board, and the drip and bedding grooves ; these are made as shown in section (Fig. 51).

To return to the pulley stiles : these must be sawn off square at the marks K and N, and the tongues formed at the top ends, H being the shoulder of the same. The pocket-pieces should be cut as in section (Fig. 52), the groove allowing the saw room to work

on the face sides, and centre-bit holes being bored
half way through at the back, as in Fig. 53, to allow
it to work there.   These holes also allow the padsaw
to enter in cutting out the pocket-pieces down the
middle of the plough groove, after which a smart
tap from the back will split them out.

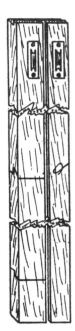

FIG. 54.—POCKET-PIECE   FIG. 55.—PULLEY STILES
WITH NAILS INSERTED.   FINISHED.

Two small nails, driven in as shown in Fig. 54,
will push the bevelled top up to a close joint, and
the pocket-pieces can be planed off level, when they
will scarcely show.   It is far better to cut them
out in this way with the saw than to use what
is called a " pocket knife," which is really a thin

chisel; of course, the finest saw available should be used.

The pulleys are inserted by boring two holes of suitable size between the marks made for them, and cutting away the wood between, so that the body of the pulley may be inserted ; it is then easy

FIG. 56.—FIXING PULLEY   FIG. 57.—PULLEY STILES
  STILES IN SILL.   FIXED TO SILL.

to mark round the flange, cut out the wood to the marks, and then screw the pulleys in.

The whole of the frame is now ready for putting together, the pulley stiles being as shown in Fig. 55. The head is first nailed to the two pulley stiles, and then the latter are placed in their respective notches in the sill, and fixed with wedges, testing them during the operation with a straight-edge, held against the inside edge of the sill, as in Fig. 56. When quite correct by the straight-edge, as above, and also out of twist, two nails should be driven through the wedges and pulley stiles, into the sill, as at R (Fig. 57), thus fixing them firmly.

The dividing tongues should be fixed next, by making a slot or a mortise in the projecting ends

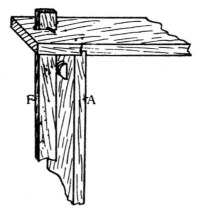

FIG. 58.—DIVIDING TONGUE FIXED TO HEAD.

of the head and fixing the tongues in them with a nail through each. These tongues should be long enough to reach to within about 3 ins. or 4 ins. of the bottom of the pocket-pieces—not longer, or they will be in the way when inserting the weights; and not shorter, or there is the risk of the weights getting under them and jamming. One corner of the frame at this stage is shown at Fig. 58.

To fix the linings, the frame, so far as it is made, is laid flat on the bench, the thick edge of the sill

(that is, the inside) uppermost; the sill is fixed
firmly to the bench by screwing a strip of wood to
both bench and sill (as S, **Fig. 59**). The frame
should then be tested diagonally across the corners,
and, when quite true, a single nail into the bench
from the upper side of the head T will keep it so

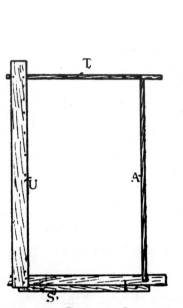

FIG. 59.—PUTTING LININGS
ON TO FRAME.

FIG. 60.—LINING CUT
READY FOR FIXING.

while the linings are nailed on. The side linings
should be fixed first—one being shown as fixed at
U (Fig. 59)—keeping them level with the face of
the pulley stile, and always remembering that no
nails must be driven into the pocket-pieces, but to
nail very firmly to both sill and head. The head

lining simply requires fitting tightly between the two sides, and nailing.

After cleaning off this side, the frame must be turned over on the bench and fixed tightly, testing it to see that it is quite square as before ; the linings

FIG. 61.—HEAD LINING CUT TO FIT SIDE LININGS.   FIG. 62.—SECTION OF WATER BEAD ON SILL.

are then laid on and marked for cutting. At the bottom end they must be bevelled on the end to fit the sill, and at the top end cut to a mitre to receive the head lining. Five-eighths of an inch must be cut away, this being the proper distance for the linings to project over the pulley stiles. One lining cut ready for fixing is shown in Fig. 60, and the head lining cut to fit it in Fig. 61.

Blocks as V (Fig. 43) should be placed across the

FIGS. 63 AND 64.—SECTIONS OF BEADED OUTSIDE LININGS.

junction of the side and head linings, as shown by dotted lines in Fig. 48, and, if the frames are more than 3 ft. wide, another block should be placed between.

The back linings are simply thin boards nailed to

the back edges of the linings, serving the double purpose of stiffening the latter and keeping out all dust and mortar.

The parting beads should be fitted while the frame is still on the bench ; also the staff beads, not forgetting the water bead on the sill, a correct section of which is given in Fig. 62.

Although the above may be taken as the average sash frame, as used in ordinary good class work, we often find certain modifications ; for instance,

FIGS. 65 AND 66.—ALTERNATIVE METHODS OF FORMING POCKET-PIECES.

in many parts of the country the outside linings are beaded, as either Figs. 63 or 64. The former adds slightly to the appearance, without making much extra work, but the latter has nothing to be said in its favour—the only thing it does is to hide badly fitting sashes, and allow the cold winds to enter.

The sills are often double-sunk, as Fig. 51 ; this is supposed to be an additional safeguard against the entrance of water ; but if the water bead is used, the double sinking is not necessary.

Some faddists cut their pocket-pieces as Figs. 65 or 66 ; but nothing can be said in favour of either. They take longer to do, use up more material and

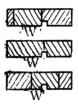

FIG. 67.—CROSS SECTIONS OF VARIOUS FORMS OF POCKET-PIECES.

cause more damage to the paint every time a sash-cord has to be renewed.

Fig. 67 shows cross-sections of the three methods of placing the pocket-pieces, the top and the bottom being as shown in Figs. 65 and 66, while the middle one is what we consider the correct method, as described above, W being the pocket-piece in each case.

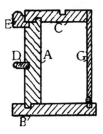

FIG. 68.—PULLEY STILES TONGUED INTO LININGS FOR VERY GOOD WORK.

In very good work the pulley stile is tongued into the linings, as in Fig. 68, or, if the outside lining is beaded, as Fig. 69. In the former case the staff

bead is also tongued into the pulley stile, and the
inside linings ploughed to receive the splayed or
other linings.

The width of the pulley stiles is always regulated
by the thickness of the sashes, but the linings are
too often regulated according to the conscience of
the builder. We have seen frames made with only
2-in. inside linings ; but there should never be less
than 3 ins.—in fact. a very good rule is in force in

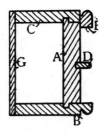

FIG. 69.—AS FIG. 68, BUT WITH BEADED OUTSIDE
LINING.

some parts to make the inside and outside lining
out of a 9-in. board, thus giving about 4 ins. and 4⅝ ins.
respectively after sawing and planing. This gives
good room for the weights.

Another great fault we often find is the making of
the pocket-pieces too short. These should range
from 15 ins., as given above, to 2 ft. in very high
frames, or trouble is likely to follow when the weights
have to be inserted.

CHAPTER IV

VERTICAL SLIDING SASHES

HAVING in the previous chapter described the making of the sash frame, we will now show how to make the sashes to fit in it. In the first place, the correct measurements must be taken : the height from under the head to the top of the sinking of the sill, as dotted line A (see Fig. 70) and also the width between the pulley stiles. The latter is simple enough, and cannot well be done any way but the right ; but the former is quite different. We have known the measurements to be taken between the head and the top part of the sill, and also down to the bottom of the sinking, as well as to the thin front edge of the sill. In the former case, the sashes of course proved to be too small, and in the latter too large, which is almost as bad, as, when so much is planed off in fitting, the haunchings are reduced, and the sashes weakened very much.

On this account, we have thought it necessary to give a sectional elevation of the frame, showing exactly where the dimensions should be taken from, so that mistakes could not be made, hence Fig. 70.

The sizes of the various parts of sashes vary very much : if the ready-worked stuff has to be used, as is usually now the case, the sizes are, of course, already settled ; but if it has to be ripped out and planed up, we can please ourselves, and suitable sizes

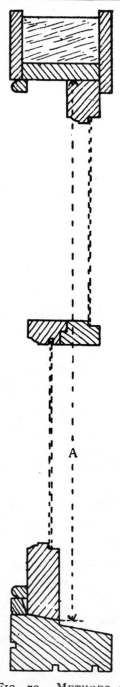

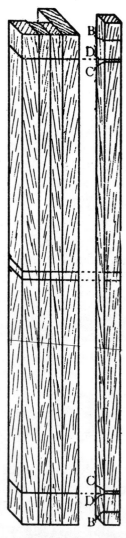

FIG. 70.—METHODS OF
MEASURING FOR SASHES.

FIG. 71.—SETTING OUT RAILS
AND BARS FROM WIDTH
ROD.

will be found to be 2¼ ins. wide for the stiles and top rail, 4½ ins. wide for the bottom rail, ¾ in. thick for the bars, and 1¼ ins. for the meeting rails.

The above sizes will cut out of the stock 9-in. deals without waste, and will make strong sashes, whether 1½ ins. or 1¾ ins. The width of the meeting rails must in any case be the same as the finished thickness of the sashes, plus the thickness of the parting beads; thus, for 1¾-in. sashes, which will hold, when finished, 1⅝ in. thick, the meeting rails must be within 1-16th in. of 2 ins. wide, and for 1½-in. sashes ¼ in. less.

Before cutting out the stuff, the rod should be set out, both width and height; the former is shown set out in Fig. 71. First make the marks B the full width of the required sashes apart; from these measure off inwards the width of the sash stiles, which, according to the remarks above, will be 2¼ ins., or, allowing for planing, 2⅛ ins., which gives us C. Then, towards B at either end, measure from C the depth to which your moulding planes work down, which will probably be from ¼ in. to 5-16ths in.; thus we obtain the two marks D. Now set out the thickness of the bars (a full ⅝ in.) midway between the marks B, which finishes this rod.

The height-rod is shown in Fig. 72 (the two should in practice be set out on different sides of the same rod). To set out, mark off the full height of the pair of sashes, as taken from the frame (as E); from this, at one end mark off 4½ ins. to F., back the depth of the moulding to G, and also 2¼ ins. from F to H.

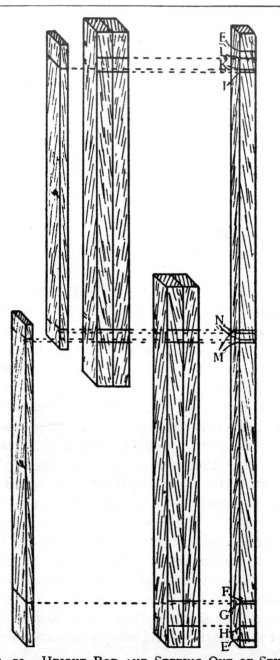

FIG. 72.—HEIGHT ROD AND SETTING OUT OF STILES
AND BARS.

At the other end mark off the width of the top rail ($2\frac{1}{8}$ ins.) to I, back the depth of the moulding to K, and also $1\frac{3}{8}$ ins. from I to L.

Now, midway between F and I set off the thickness of the meeting rails ($1\frac{1}{4}$ ins.) for marks M, and the depth of the moulding from each of these for marks N.

In marking off the stuff, all the rails should be cut $\frac{1}{2}$ in. longer than the width of the sashes, while the stiles should be cut about $4\frac{1}{2}$ ins. longer than the height as shown by the rod. This applies to the stiles for both sashes, which vary in length, owing to the difference in width between the bottom and top rails.

In planing up the stuff, it should be done so that the moulding and rebate will work with the grain, and not against it. This can be easily managed by reversing each piece as required when facing it up.

The rails are set out as in Fig. 71. Lay the bottom rail on the bench, face upwards; on this the meeting rail for the bottom sash, face downwards; next, the meeting rail for the top sash, face up; and then the top rail, face down, keeping all the face edges towards you, and all level. The rod can now be laid on the top rail, and the marks D squared across them, using chisel or knife; the two marks for the bar mortises must also be squared across at the same time. These latter must be also squared down at the back of the top and bottom rails, marking for the wedging at the same time; and across on each side of the meeting rails; also marking for wedging on the side opposite to the face. The meeting rails should be marked so that they can be identified as top and bottom, as, if they get reversed, it will throw the bars out of upright, unless set out very truly indeed.

The shoulder marks D must be squared across at each side of all the rails, and also on the opposite edge of the *top* meeting rail only, the reason for which will appear later on.

Now for the stiles, of which those for the top and bottom sashes must be set out separately. Place a pair of the latter on the bench with the face marks opposite each other. Lay the rod on them so that nearly all of the extra length on the stiles comes at the meeting rail end; then transfer the marks F and H at one end, and the two marks M at the other, to them, as in Fig. 72. Square these across and mark for the wedging, as shown.

The bar for the bottom sash is set out by transferring the mark G for the shoulders at one end; but at the meeting rail end the shoulder at the face edge is marked from N, and the outside shoulder from M.

The stiles for the top sash are set out in the same way, the mortises for the top rail being given by the marks I and L, and for the meeting rail by M, both being squared over and marked for wedging, as before.

The bar for the top sash is also set out in the same way as for the bottom one—M being the shoulder line for the top rail, and M and N the inside and outside shoulder lines respectively (see Fig. 72). It will be noticed that where the bars come to the meeting rails the shoulders are reversed, the bottom bar having the longer shoulder on the *inside*, to allow of scribing to the moulding on the meeting rail of the bottom sash, and the outside shoulder cut short, owing to the meeting rail not being rebated, whereas the meeting rail of the top sash is rebated, and not moulded ; thus the bar must have the long shoulder outside, and the short one inside. A glance at the

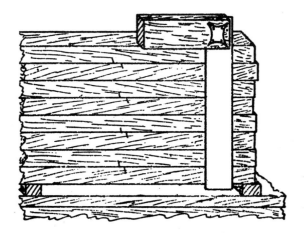

FIG. 73.—SETTING OUT NUMBER OF STILES AT ONE TIME.

section of meeting rails in Fig. 70 will make this quite plain. It is really very simple, but there are few beginners who have not made mistakes in cutting these bars.

When more than one pair of sashes are being made, all the stiles, rails, bars, etc., will be set out in batches, thus saving much squaring over. A pile of stiles is shown in Fig. 73, as being set out together, and it is easy to see that much time is saved by simply squaring over the top one, and squaring all down at the back for the mortises. By this method we are also certain of getting all exactly alike.

The gauging for mortises and tenons, cutting of the shoulders on the bars, sticking the mouldings and rebates, and cutting of the haunchings and scribings, will be the same as described in Chap. II, so that we can pass this over, except as concerns the meeting rails, and the bars which come to them.

FIG. 74.—MEETING RAIL FOR BOTTOM SASH, WITH SHOULDERS CUT.

First, as to the meeting rails : the bottom one must be gauged with the mortise gauge in the same way as the stiles, etc. ; it must also be gauged with a marking gauge, set to the thickness of the stiles, so that instead of having two shoulders, it will have one shoulder at the face edge and a slot mortise at the place corresponding with the outside shoulder on the bottom rail. This rail must also be ploughed with about $\frac{1}{4}$ in. groove, instead of being rebated, the groove coinciding with the edge of the rebates on the stiles ; and, lastly, after the moulding is stuck and the groove made, it must be rebated away for half of its thickness at the outside edge, but on the face side. Now, when the shoulders are cut and the slot mortises mentioned above knocked out, the end of the rail will appear as Fig. 74.

The meeting rail on the top sash must not be gauged in the same way as the other, but the head

FIG. 75.—MEETING RAIL FOR TOP SASH, WITH SHOULDERS CUT.

of the gauge must be shifted the thickness of the parting bead, thus throwing the tenon so much nearer the outside edge of the rail. This latter must also be gauged from the *outside* edge, using the above-mentioned marking gauge as it is already set, which will give the slot mortise in place of the inside shoulder. No moulding must be stuck on this rail, and before sticking the rebate the fillester must be shifted to correspond with the mortise gauge, thus bringing the rebate to the side of the tenon, and the same width as those on the stiles. Lastly, the rail must be rebated on the inside edge, cutting away half the thickness from the face side, and then, after cutting the shoulders, etc., we have Fig. 75.

Now to finish the bars; the top one requires no scribing, but is simply left square—shouldered—as Fig. 76, but the bottom one must be scribed, when it will be as Fig. 77.

The ends of the stiles should be finished with

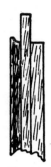

Fig. 76.—Bar for Top Sash.   Fig. 77.—Bar for Bottom Sash.

brackets, cramping up all the stiles and working all at once, two patterns of which are shown in Figs. 78 and 79. These figures also show how the moulding is manipulated at the meeting rails—the one for the top sash being cut off square with the mortise (as in Fig. 78), so that it fits on the level surface of the meeting rail; while the bottom one is cut away only to allow of scribing in the ordinary way (as in Fig. 79).

The same two figures show also how the sashes can be made much stronger with little trouble;

a method which has been used successfully many times, but which does not seem to be adopted to any great extent, probably on account' of the extra trouble involved. This improvement consists of allowing a portion of the solid part of the meeting rails to fit in recesses cut away for the purpose in the stiles (as at O, Figs. 78 and 79), the meeting rails to suit being cut as Figs. 80 and 81.

To do the above properly, the stiles must be

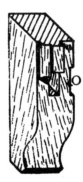

FIGS. 78 AND 79.—ALTERNATIVE SHAPE OF BRACKETS FOR STILES OF TOP SASH.

squared over from the mortise lines—the top ones on the face side, the bottom on the outside. And instead of setting the marking gauge already mentioned to the thickness of the sashes, it is set to $\frac{1}{8}$ in. less, and not only the meeting rails gauged with it, but the stiles as well, with the result that when both are cut to the marks a good fit is a certainty. And in the matter of strength, there is no comparison of the one method with the other, while the expenditure of half an hour will cover the extra work, and

we can say, from experience, that the " game "
is certainly well " worth the candle."

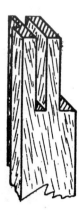

FIGS. 80 AND 81.—IMPROVED JOINT BETWEEN MEETING
RAILS AND STILES.

A few more words, and we have finished with this
particular form of sash. It is very probable that
exception may be taken by some readers to the
section of meeting rails shown, because they are not
the same as are used in some localities. We show, in

FIGS. 82 AND 83.—ALTERNATIVE METHODS OF FITTING
TOP AND BOTTOM MEETING RAILS TOGETHER.

Figs. 82 and 83, two alternative sections, of which
the former is in more general use ; but the latter is

the better of the two for every reason, except the
one which makes the former so common—that is,
it is easy to do and no exactness is required. Consequently, we often find a space of a $\frac{1}{4}$ in. or more
between the two rails when the window is closed and
fastened ; anyone can open it from the outside,
and much dust and no slight draught is admitted.
Fig. 83 is not so much open to these objections ;
but it is more difficult to work than the style we
have shown, and not nearly so effective, either as
a draught preventer or as a window which cannot
be opened from outside.

CHAPTER V

Horizontal Sliding Sashes and Frame

THE horizontal sliding sashes are, as a rule, only found locally—that is to say, the only districts in which they are used are usually far from large towns ; and as it is in such purely country districts where new ideas are not readily accepted, it follows, that what we find in common use can only be described as old-fashioned ; therefore, we can safely say that these kind of windows are old in style, and as the craze now is for anything old, they may safely be used, especially as they are very convenient in some respects, and not particularly liable to get out of order. There is, however, one very great inconvenience connected with these windows as usually made and as shown in the drawings, which is this —one sash being a fixture, the other one, when the window is opened, is covered on the outside, making it impossible to clean it from the inside. This drawback may be removed by using three or four lights, instead of the two, as shown, and allowing the two outside ones, or alternate ones, as the case may be, to slide, which will allow anyone to get at the outsides of all by sitting on the sill and reaching round in the usual way.

The frame for this kind of window is made solid, the material being of the right width to take the two sashes, the parting bead, and the inside staff bead. An outside lining is planted on all round the frame (except the sill, which is wide enough to take it), and projects beyond the solid part ⅝ in. on the inside, thus forming the rebate for the fixed sash.   These linings should be mitred at the top angles, and notched over the sill at the bottom, in the same way as a boxed sash frame, as shown in Fig. 84, at A and B respectively.

The solid jambs and head are ploughed to take

FIG. 84.—ELEVATION OF SLIDING SASH FRAME.

the parting beads, which, in conjunction with the outside lining and the inside staff beads, form grooves to receive the outside fixed sash and the inside sliding sash, respectively.   In setting out these grooves, too much play for the sashes should not be allowed, or the draught will find its way in ; barely 1-16th in. is ample.

The sill is not ploughed to receive a parting bead, but a groove is made in it in such a position that the bottom rail of the sliding sash, when in position, will be immediately over it, and in this groove is fitted a tongue of hardwood for the sliding sash to run on.

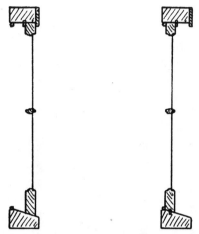

FIGS. 85 AND 86.—VERTICAL SECTIONS THROUGH FIXED AND SLIDING SASHES.

The staff beads are mitred round the frame on the inside, and fixed at such a distance from the parting beads as to allow the sliding sash to work freely.

We do not think it necessary to show how to set out the rod for this window, it being very simple to do, and almost like the casement window, as far

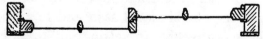

FIG. 87.—HORIZONTAL SECTION OF SLIDING SASH WINDOW.

as setting out is concerned, and all parts are clearly shown in the vertical sections through the fixed and sliding sashes, Figs. 85 and 86 ; and the horizontal section in Fig. 87 ; the details being shown on a larger scale in Figs. 88 and 89, sections of sill at outside and inside sash respectively ; and Fig. 90 section of jamb and sliding sash.

The sashes, at first sight, appear as ordinary

FIGS. 88 AND 89.—ENLARGED SECTIONS OF SILL WITH FIXED AND SLIDING SASHES.

casements ; but they are not so, as a glance at Fig. 87 will show. The two middle stiles—that is, the two which come together in the centre—instead of being formed the same as the others, are as the meeting rails in the up-and-down sashes described in Chap. IV ; and this makes them somewhat confusing to make for those who attempt them for the first time. The section of the meeting stile on the sliding sash must always be the same as that of the meeting rail in the bottom sash in the ordinary

FIG. 90.—SECTION OF JAMB OF FRAME AND SLIDING SASH.

window, the stile on the fixed sash corresponding to the rail on the top sash ; thus the glass in the latter will fit in the rebate, while that in the former will slip into a groove.

In Fig. 91 we show the bottom end of the meeting stile of the sliding sash mortised to receive the tenon of the bottom rail, which is shown in Fig. 92; and it will be noticed that the inside shoulder of the latter is left longer to scribe to the moulding on the stile, the outside shoulder having no corresponding rebate to fit to. On the other hand, the rails of the fixed sash must have the outside shoulders left the longer, as there is no moulding on the inside to scribe to.

The outside sash must be fitted so that it is tight

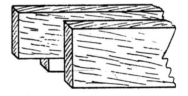

FIG. 91.—BOTTOM END OF MEETING STILE OF SLIDING SASH.

FIG. 92.—BOTTOM RAIL, TENONED TO FIT FIG. 91.

to the sill when in the groove at the jamb, and it is fixed by inserting a small nail at top and bottom through the meeting stile, and into the head and sill.

The sliding sash is fitted loosely, and the bottom rail is ploughed to suit the hardwood tongue mentioned above, but not deep enough to allow the rail to touch the sill, the secret of the easy working of these sashes depending on the tongue taking the whole weight of the sash; they will then slide back and forth easily and smoothly. But let them touch the sill, and they will jam and bind, and nothing will make them work except to put in a wider tongue.

The usual fastening for these sashes is the ordinary sash fastener, fixed on the inside of the meeting stile of the fixed sash, and springing down into the catch fixed on to the corresponding stile of the sliding sash.

If windows are made with more than the two sashes, as mentioned above, the whole of the meeting stiles should be as shown in the drawings, the sashes being inside and outside alternately, the inner ones only being made to slide, all the outer ones to be fixed. It is quite possible to make the outside sashes to slide by having another hardwood tongue, and making a groove in the bottom rail ; but the tongue makes a receptacle for water after every shower of rain, and the sill will soon be rotten.

If very heavy sashes are made in this style, the tongues may wear away fast, and make the sashes work badly ; if so, a pair of pulleys may be inserted in the bottom rail, with grooved wheels to run on the tongue. The stamped steel frame pulleys do well in this connection, being cheap, easily fixed, and as near everlasting as it is possible to be. The tongue should be rounded on the top edge to fit the grooved wheel, or a piece of round-edged iron bar may be used instead of the tongue. Do not, on any account, use flat iron and ordinary sash rollers, or even the latter running on the wood sill, without the tongue. This latter acts as a very effective draught excluder, besides forming the runner for the sash.

CHAPTER VI

THE BAY WINDOW

BAY windows may be, and often are, formed by means of three ordinary sash frames, the angles at the junction of these being of brick or stone. In such as this, the bay is formed by the way in which the windows are placed, and it is not really an independent bay window, and, therefore, does not concern us here.

A complete bay window is made entirely of woodwork, and although it is made really out of three separate frames, yet these must be so built up together as to form a strong and substantial whole. Thus, the only real difference in the construction of the bay and the ordinary sash frame lies in the joining of the sills, heads, and linings at the angles.

We may remark, in passing, that the correct angle for the sides from the front is one of 45 degs. This is at times departed from for certain reasons, often unintentionally or through ignorance of the method to be adopted to obtain the correct angle ; but the fact remains that in nearly every case the " true mitre," as it is usually termed, is what is wanted.

The plan of a bay window is shown in Fig. 93, and the corresponding elevation in Fig. 94, and from these it may be seen that the only difference in the construction lies in the joining of the sills and linings, as mentioned above. The former is the most important, and we will deal with this first. Various methods are used, as the plain mitre (Fig. 95),

FIG. 93.—PLAN OF BAY WINDOW.

the halving (Fig. 96), the mortise and tenon (Fig. 97), and the dovetail key (Fig. 98).

It is difficult to say which is the best of these, though probably it will be hard to beat the mortise and tenon (Fig. 97) for strength : but it is somewhat

FIG. 94.—ELEVATION OF BAY WINDOW.

tedious to do, and must be done properly or it is of no use. The most simple is the plain mitre ; but as this depends for its strength entirely on nails

or screws, it is not to be recommended, except for
the commonest kind of work.

The halving (Fig. 96) is very good, the screws

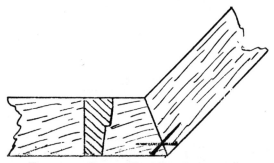

FIG. 95.—SILLS MITRED AT ANGLES.

holding the joints up tightly; but they require
to be inserted in the same way as draw-boring is
done, or the chances are that the mitre at the front
will not draw up close. The mortise and tenon
(**Fig. 97**) is the best, as it may be draw-bored properly.
The tenon should be shaped as shown by dotted

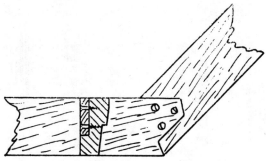

FIG. 96.—SILLS HALVED AT ANGLES.

lines, and it will readily be seen that the mortise is
somewhat difficult to make, owing to the cutting
against the grain.

The dovetail key joint (Fig. 98) is easy to make, being simply a plain mitre, and the double dovetail key fitted in after, the fixing being done with screws.

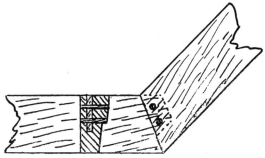

FIG. 97.—SILLS MORTISED AND TENONED TOGETHER.

All the fitting of the sills must be done before the recesses are cut away to receive the linings, as, if this is done first, it is difficult to make the parts intersect.

As a guide in getting the proper angles to the sills, a template should be made by screwing boards together, and the sills set out on this to the full size

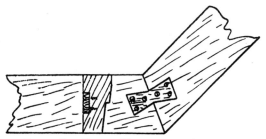

FIG. 98.—SILLS KEYED AT ANGLES.

and width; the various parts can then be laid on this template while fitting them, ensuring correct angles.

The heads are put together in the same way as
the sills ; but, as they are covered by the linings,
there is no need to mitre the outside, the halving
may be cut quite through, as Fig. 99 ; or, if tenoned,
the tenons and mortises may be of the "slot"

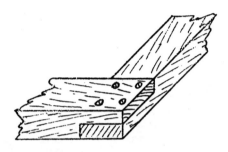

FIG. 99.—METHOD OF JOINING HEAD AT ANGLES.

variety. Sometimes, instead of using the ordinary
cased heads, solid heads are used, the outside
lining only being nailed on, as shown in Fig. 100.
This method facilitates the putting together of
the bay, making the frame stronger at the corners,
and the only difference it makes in the construction is—the head requires cutting away on the

FIG. 100.—SOLID HEAD WITH LINING NAILED ON.

inside, to take the linings, in the same way as the
sills.

The notches to receive the pulley stiles must not
be made until the fitting together has been done,
and it is as well not to make them wider than

necessary, so as to leave as much strength as possible for the wedging.

The notches for pulley stiles and the recesses for linings having been cut, the sills and heads may

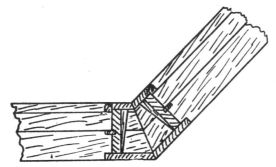

FIG. 101.—METHOD OF FIXING AND FITTING LININGS
TOGETHER.

be fixed together permanently, and the pulley stiles wedged in in the usual way, and the head nailed on ; after which comes the fixing of the linings. These should be fixed on the inside first, mitreing the two at the angles, as in Fig. 101 (also shown enlarged in Fig. 102) ; or, what is a better way, lapping one on

FIGS. 102 AND 103.—ALTERNATIVE METHODS OF FITTING
INSIDE LININGS.

the other, as in Fig. 103. The advantage of the latter lies in the fact that the two can be fixed together from the back, thus giving the two pieces no chance of squeezing past each other and leaving an open joint. The outside linings can be mitred together, and also bradded, but even then the joint is apt to open ; and it is often covered entirely by fixing a half-round rod up the angle, as in Fig. 104.

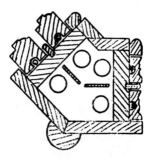

FIG. 104.—SECTION OF ANGLE OF BAY, WITH HALF-ROUND MOULDING FIXED.

The pulley stiles should all have pulleys inserted, so that all the sashes can be opened ; but this is sometimes omitted, the side sashes being fixed. These should not be fixed too tightly, as they often have to be removed.   The best fixing for the top sash

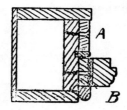

FIG. 105.—METHOD OF FIXING SASHES.

is to fit a thin piece between the outside lining and the .parting bead tightly under the sash, bradding it in with two or three brads only ; or, better still, fixing it with about two screws, as at A (Fig. 105).

The bottom sash is best fixed by screwing through the stile brackets into the pulley stiles, as at B (Fig. 105). In preparing the pulley stiles there is no need to make pocket pieces in both at the

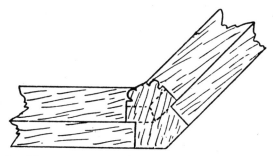

FIG. 106.—METHOD OF TENONING SILLS AND HEAD INTO JAMBS FOR BAY CASEMENT FRAMES.

angles, as both weights can be taken out from the centre.

In making bay *casement* frames, the strongest method is to let the angle stile run down and tenon the heads and sills into it, as shown in Figs. 106 and 107 ; but, in doing this, the angle stiles must

FIG. 107.—ELEVATION OF FIG. 106.

be prepared to exactly the right bevel, or the angle will be a long way out. This necessity is often the cause of the other method being adopted, as being easier to keep right in this respect.

Before leaving the present subject, we would remark that in putting the sills and heads together, the tenons or halvings should be painted, also the pins, and any screws used should be greased; this makes them go in easier, and also prevents rust. This is, of course, assuming that oak is used for sills; if these are of deal, no greasing of screws will be required.

CHAPTER VII

Venetian Windows

VENETIAN, or as they were sometimes called, marginal light, windows were very fashionable at one time, indeed it looked as though they might replace the bay window, although the same style was sometimes adapted to the bay instead of the original up and down sliding sashes. These Venetian windows are, as may be gathered from the drawings, of the casement variety, and the sashes should be made to open outwards if possible, this being the better way to keep out the wet.

In Fig. 108 we show one of these windows fitted with four lights or casements, the two outside ones being hinged to the jambs, and the two middle ones, which fold together, being hinged in like manner to the mullions. The casements in this frame run from sill to head, the upper part being divided into small squares as shown, which is the simplest way of forming an artistic window.

Another method of filling in these window frames is shown in Fig. 110, which shows the filling between the mullions. Here the casements are in two heights, the bottom pair being hinged in the ordinary way to the mullions ; the other, which is wide enough to fill the whole space, is hinged at the top, and opens outwards, the bottom rail of this fitting to the others either as section, Figs. 111 or 112. The former is the simplest way and least liable to get out of order, but the latter is best as regards the keeping out of wind and water; but when the window has been repainted a few times it is apt to work badly.

Windows made in this way are very convenient, as it is possible to have the top only open, or the whole, as required. The folding casements in either

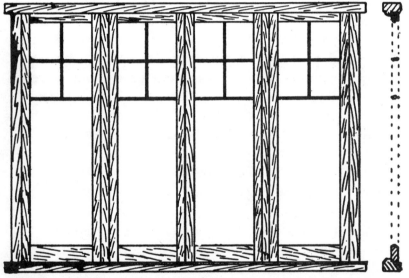

FIGS. 108 AND 109.—ELEVATION AND SECTION OF COMPLETE WINDOW.

style of window come together with a rebated joint, as Fig. 113.

Suitable sections for head and sill for these frames are shown in Fig. 114, the grooves in the latter being to form a cement key under, and to take the window board. It will also be noticed that the bevel of the sill finishes with a hollow, forming an undercut rebate; this should not be omitted, owing to its use

as a water trap. The same also applies to the
groove in the bottom rail of the casement, which
tends to the same purpose. In these windows the
jambs are the same in section as the head, and the
mullions the same, but worked both sides; thus
there is no need to give sectional illustrations of
these.

Fig. 115 shows a window of a more ambitious

FIG. 110.—ALTERNATIVE METHOD OF FILLING IN WITH
CASEMENTS.

kind, and which is not strictly Venetian, though
often called so. In addition to the mullions, as in
the former example, the present window is divided
in height by the insertion of a transom. A half-
sectional plan of this window is given in Fig. 116
(this will also serve the same purpose for Fig. 108,
both being alike in this respect), and a vertical
section in Fig. 117. In these sections the whole of

the framing is flush at both sides, the sashes being kept back from the face sufficiently far to allow of a somewhat heavy chamfer being run round, as shown in Fig. 118, but the frame is improved if the transome and sill is made to project as in the section (Fig. 119). This is also an additional safeguard against the wet, the projections allowing of a water groove being made underneath, as shown.

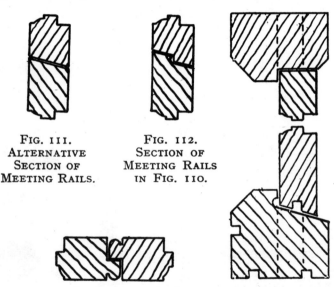

FIG. 111.
ALTERNATIVE
SECTION OF
MEETING RAILS.

FIG. 112.
SECTION OF
MEETING RAILS
IN FIG. 110.

FIG. 113.
SECTION OF MEETING STILES
(FIG. 108).

FIG. 114.
ENLARGED SECTIONS
OF FIG. 108.

Fig. 119 also shows an alternative moulding on the inside of the frame, in place of the chamfer shown in Fig. 114, and in many cases the transom is made use of to introduce more or less elaborate mouldings. These, however, make no difference as regards method of making, though it may do in the setting out, which must in every case be dealt with according to requirements.

In Fig. 120 we show the rod for setting out the

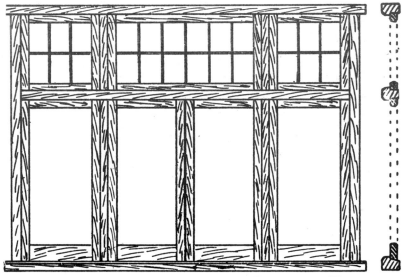

FIGS. 115 AND 117.—ELEVATION AND SECTION OF WINDOW WITH TRANSOM FRAMED IN

frame of the window shown in Fig. 115, which, for the sake of illustration, is 8 ft. wide by 6 ft. high outside, the framing throughout being $4\frac{1}{2}$ ins. wide by 4 ins. thick. The width of the frame is on the side of the rod marked A, the marks B show the

FIG. 116.—PART HORIZONTAL SECTION OF FIGS. 108 AND 115.

full width of frame, outside. From B to C, inwards, should be the thickness of the framing after it is planed up, which will probably be $\frac{1}{8}$ in. under the

4 ins., and from C to D, outwards, is the depth of
the rebate. From C at each end set off the width
of the side lights, or, rather, the distance from
jamb to mullion, and the thickness of the framing
again, which gives us E and F, and from these
mark off the depth of the re-
bates again, thus getting G.

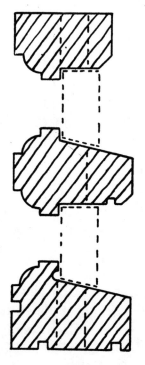

In setting out the stuff from
the rod, the marks D and G
will be for the mortises, these
coming in the rebates, as shown
by dotted lines in Fig. 119, and
if the sashes have to come flush
with the framing outside the
same marks will be the shoulder
lines for the transom on the
outside edge. The dotted lines

FIG. 118.—SECTION OF
MOULDED MULLION, WITH
SASH STILES.

FIG. 119.—SECTION OF
SILL, TRANSOM, AND
HEAD OF FIG. 115.

on the rod will be the shoulder lines for the inside of
the transom, and also for the outside, if the framing
is allowed to project, and is chamfered as in Fig. 118.

The height rod is set out on the side marked H,
the lines I showing the full height, 6 ft.   K is the

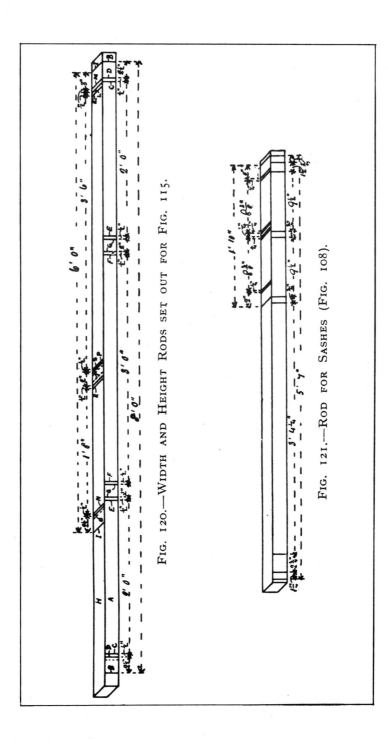

FIG. 120.—WIDTH AND HEIGHT RODS SET OUT FOR FIG. 115.

FIG. 121.—ROD FOR SASHES (FIG. 108).

thickness of the sill, then L and M for the depth of rebate and the bevel respectively, the latter being made to correspond with the inside chamfer.

From I at the top set off the thickness of the framing and back the depth of the rebate, thus getting N and O respectively. Now measure up the height of the bottom casements from K, set off the thickness of the framing above this, and back from each, $\frac{1}{2}$ in. for depth of rebate, and again from the top one of these for the bevel on transome. This gives us the marks P, R, and S, respectively.

In setting out this from rod, the marks M and O are the shoulder lines at sill and head on the outside, L giving the angle in the former, while S will be the shoulder lines for the mullion under the transome. T is the same above the transome, and the line between R and T gives the angle.

The shoulder lines on the inside are the same as M and T at the sill and upper side of the transom, and as dotted lines under the latter, and at the head.

The rod for setting out of the sashes of Fig. 118 is given in Fig. 121, and as this is simply the same as what is met with in ordinary windows, no detailed description is necessary, the sizes marked on being sufficient.

ELEMENTARY
STAIRCASING

THE PRINCIPLES AND METHODS OF CONSTRUCTION
CLEARLY DESCRIBED

CONTENTS

Elementary Staircasing

CHAPTER I

How to Set Out and Make a Step-Ladder

Although, perhaps, strictly speaking, a step-ladder cannot be called a staircase, yet it is certainly a stairs, therefore it may well be taken as the first step towards the more ambitious form which follows after, and as the setting out and making up must be on the same principle throughout, we make no apology for including this in the present handbook.

As it is quite possible there may be some of our readers who have a very hazy idea as to what is meant by a step-ladder, we will, before showing how to make it, give a short explanation of what it really is.

A step-ladder is the same as an ordinary ladder, except that, instead of the slight side pieces and the round staves (or rungs), the sides (technically " strings ") are made from scantling, and the place of the staves is filled by flat " treads." Thus it will be seen that a step-ladder is stronger and safer than a ladder, and, owing to the flat " treads," it must be made correct to measurement for the place it has to fill; otherwise, instead of these being flat (level), they will form so many inclined planes more or less dangerous to walk up or down, according to the degree of inclination.

The attainment of a perfectly level tread depends, in the first place, upon finding the correct length of the strings, and, secondly, on the treads being placed in the strings at the correct angle. By working on a correct principle, each of these conditions will fulfil themselves; and we cannot do better than

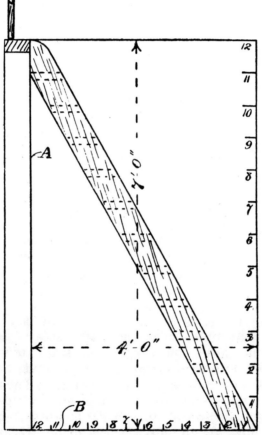

FIG. I.—SIDE ELEVATION OF STEP-LADDER.

illustrate by means of a practical example what is the correct principle to work on.

Fig. I herewith shows a side elevation of a step-ladder in use as a means of reaching an outside doorway on the first floor of a building. The height from the ground line to the top of the door sill is 7 ft., and, therefore, this is the height we wish to reach with our step-ladder. The next factor to determine is the space the bottom of the step-ladder has to start from. This may be confined, or it may not ; if it is, we must work to the fixed space, always remembering that room must be allowed at the foot, quite clear of the bottom step, for a person to start mounting from—say 18 ins. at the least. On the other hand, if room is plentiful, the spread of the strings should be regulated according to what the

Fig. 2.—Portion of Finished Step-ladder, Treads trenched through.

ladder is likely to be used for ; the greater the slope, the easier it will be to walk up. In the drawing we show the bottom of the strings as standing out from the wall 4 ft.—or, technically speaking, 4 ft. " going." Now, to obtain the correct angle for the treads, we have only to set out to scale on board or paper the vertical line A, and the horizontal line B ; making a mark at 7 ft. and 4 ft. from the angle respectively, then connecting the two diagonally will give the slope of the strings ; and a bevel set to the angle formed by the diagonal and the horizontal line is the line of the treads required. (See dotted tread lines in the drawing, Fig. 1.)

The next thing is to ascertain the number of treads required. Thus, 7 ft. divided by 12 gives us 7 ins., which is a good rise for easy mounting, and will mean that we shall want eleven treads, the door sill forming the top one, as shown by the numbers at the right hand of the drawing. Each tread will be 4 ins. in front of the one above it (4 ft. divided by 12 giving 4 ins.), as shown on the horizontal line at the bottom of the drawing. The length of the strings can be roughly ascertained by means of the diagonal line, but they should be cut

FIG. 3.—PORTION OF FINISHED STEP-LADDER, ALTERNATIVE METHOD.

off a few inches longer than this, to be cut exactly when finished.

There are two methods of attaching the treads to the strings. In both cases they are trenched in, but in the one case the trenches are made quite through the width of the strings, the treads coming to both front and back, as in Fig. 2. The alternative method is to have the treads less in width, but thicker, and not to trench right through the strings; this is shown in Fig. 3 and Fig. 5, and we consider it the better method of the two. The strings being kept intact at both edges leaves them stronger; and although the trenches take somewhat longer to make

the extra labour is amply repaid by results. A
portion of one string trenched for each of the above
methods is shown in Figs. 4 and 5 respectively, from
which each may be judged on its merits.

Fig. 6 shows the method of setting out the strings.
First mark the edges which are intended for the top,
as shown (the convex edge should be kept at the
top if the strings are not quite straight) ; then by
means of the bevel make the mark C, which will fit

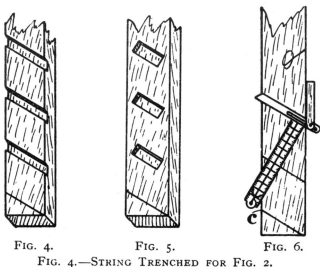

FIG. 4.   FIG. 5.   FIG. 6.

FIG. 4.—STRING TRENCHED FOR FIG. 2.
FIG. 5.—STRING TRENCHED FOR FIG. 3.
FIG. 6.—METHOD OF SETTING OUT STRINGS.

to the ground line. Measure up from this the rise
required, and make the second mark ; and so on
until the number required is reached, the last one
representing the extreme top of the ladder, no tread
being wanted. In setting out as above, the rule
must be kept at exact right angles to the blade of
the bevel, as in the drawing, otherwise the measurements will vary ; and it is best to have the two
strings laid side by side, face edges towards each

other, and to set both out at once, thus avoiding mistakes.

We have so far one mark only on the strings, showing the position of the top side of each tread. To find the width of the trenches, each separate tread should be marked in and numbered, thus ensuring a tight fit, without the trouble of gauging the treads to thickness. If the method shown in Fig. 2 is being used, the treads are simply stood on the string, while the bottom comes level with the front edge ; but if, as recommended, the alternative method has been adopted, a mark should be made on the inside of the string at about ¾ in. from the

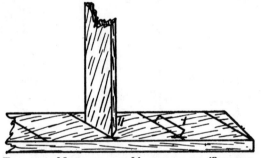

FIG. 7.—METHOD OF MARKING IN TREADS.

face edge, and each tread placed to this mark while scribing the trenching. Each tread should be numbered on the under side as marked in, the string being marked in a corresponding manner. Fig. 7 shows the first tread as marked in and numbered, the second one being in position for marking and already numbered. After all are marked in, the trenches must be cut to an equal depth throughout, and holes bored through from the trenches outwards to take the nails to be used in fixing together.

To do this, lay one string down, trenches upwards, drive all the treads in, then place the other string on them, and drive on in place, fixing with nails.

The whole can then be turned over, and the other
string nailed on. We should mention that the
treads must be sawn off to the required length,
quite square at the ends, and then there will be no
difficulty in making the step-ladder square, otherwise this will be an utter impossibility.

FIG. 8.—TREAD DOUBLE
TENONED.

FIG. 9.—TREAD SINGLE
TENONED.

To refer back to Fig. 1, it will be noticed that at
the top end the strings are not cut off at the 4-in.
width of tread, as would seem strictly correct, but
allowed about 2 ins. wider. This is as it should be
owing to the solid wall at this point, which would
otherwise give very little room for foothold. This

FIG. 10.—TEMPLATE FOR
SETTING OUT DOUBLE TENON
AND MORTISE.

FIG. 11.—TEMPLATE FOR
SINGLE TENON AND
MORTISE.

constitutes one of the pitfalls which the inexperi-
enced are liable to fall into.

In making very long step-ladders it is best to
allow one or more of the treads near the middle,
as well as the next but one on the top and bottom,
to pass through the strings in the form of one or
two tenons, which tenons should be parallel with

the strings—not at right angles to the tread—thus appearing as Figs. 8 or 9. This tenon being bevelled is somewhat awkward to set out, both as tenon and

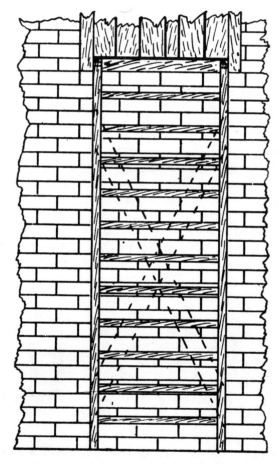

FIG. 12.—FRONT ELEVATION OF STEP-LADDER IN POSITION.

mortise ; this, however, may be got over by making a template as either Fig. 10 or Fig. 11, from which both the tenons and mortises may be easily marked, with a certainty of their being a good fit. The

method of fixing in these tenoned treads is by
wedging from the outside, and placing the wedges
across the grain of the strings ; or, if the latter ar
very thick, the treads may be pinned in as well.
The trenching is not dispensed with, even though
the treads are tenoned, as the latter is really more
to prevent the strings from spreading than to take
the weight of the traffic on the ladder. In making
a very long step-ladder, the strings should be stiffened
by screwing on diagonal braces at the back, as
shown by dotted lines in Fig. 12.

Nothing has been said as to suitable sizes of
timber to use. This, of course, varies according to
circumstances, and may range from 4-in. by 1½-in.
string with 3-in. by 1-in. treads, to 8-in. by 4-in.
strings and 7-in. by 2-in. treads ; but experience is
the best teacher in this respect. For a step-ladder
as shown in the drawings used as a means of getting
to the upper floor of a farm building, we would
recommend 6-in. by 2-in. strings and 5-in. by 1½-in.
treads, if made in hardwood (oak preferably, as it
would be outside) ; but if made in deal, the materials
should be stouter, the strings in width and the treads
in thickness.

CHAPTER II

A Cottage Staircase

WITH the present chapter we enter on our subject proper, dealing with the setting out of a straight flight of stairs such as is found in a somewhat cheap style of cottage.

Before describing the method of doing this, we

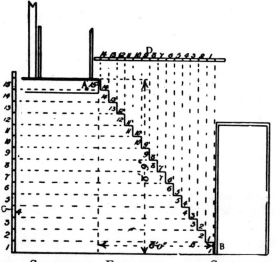

FIG. 13.—SECTIONAL ELEVATION OF STAIRCASE, WITH "HEIGHT" AND "GOING" RODS.

would like to disarm criticism as to the extreme dimensions of the steps of the stairs, which we have adopted, this being done with a special object, which will appear later on, otherwise we should have modified the dimensions considerably. To take a case in point, we will suppose that we have to make a flight of stairs to reach the first floor of a cottage, in which the rooms are of 8-ft. pitch—thus, including the width of joists and thickness of floor we have to get up to the height of 8 ft. 9 ins., while the space we have to do this in is limited to the distance from the front of the landing A to the stairfoot doorway B (Fig. 13) which is 6 ft. Thus, in technical terms, our stairs must be of 8-ft. 9-in. rise by 6-ft. going, and the former dimension must be divided into a certain number of spaces to obtain the height of each riser, the latter being divided in the same way to get the width of the tread.

This dividing of the rise and going is best done (in the case of a novice especially) on strips of wood, these being shown in the drawing at C and D, respectively. By using these strips of wood the

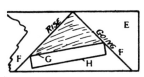

Fig. 14.—Method of Setting
out Step-board.

Fig. 15.—Step-board
Complete.

dividing may be done with the compasses, which will come easier than doing it by figures only, especially when it comes out to minute parts of an inch.

In the drawing we have divided the height into 15 risers, which brings them to 7 ins. exactly, and the going to correspond with this must be divided into 14 only, which gives $5\frac{1}{8}$ ins., or near enough to this for practical purposes.

The rods set out as above, the next thing is to make the step- (or pitch-) board. This is done as follows : Take a piece of sound $\frac{1}{2}$-in. board as E (Fig. 14), and on it make the two lines F at right angles to each other as shown. On one of these set off the rise and on the other the going, according to the rods, and make the mark G connecting the two points, and finally, at 2 ins. from this latter line and parallel with it, make the line H.

The board must now' be cut along the lines F and H, the ends of the latter being cut off at right angles from the points formed by F and G. The sawn edges must be planed quite square, and then a piece of stuff about 2 ins. wide can be nailed on to H, leaving the finished board as Fig. 15.

The length of the boards required for the strings may be roughly ascertained by measuring the distance from point to point, along the line G, and multiplying this by the number of steps in the stairs, or, rather, by the number of risers. If cut

FIG. 16.—METHOD OF USING STEP-BOARD IN SETTING OUT STRINGS.

off to this length there will be a few inches over and above the actual requirements, to allow for scribing and fitting afterwards.

The method of applying the step-board in setting out the strings is shown in Fig. 16. The two strings, after being planed on one side and the face edge (that is the top) planed straight, should be laid on the bench face side up, and face edges toward each other, when each step is marked by means of the board, as shown at I. A knife or chisel should be used in marking, as it is the front of the riser and the top of the tread which is represented by the marks made, so that a good fit should be the first requirement.

The drawing (Fig. 16) shows the bottom ends of the strings, and these should be left slightly longer than the actual height of the riser, to allow of scribing

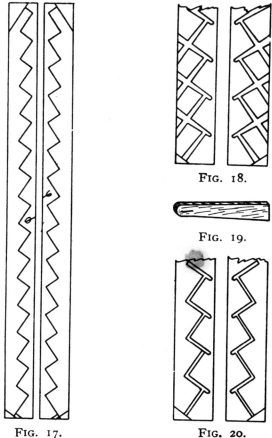

FIG. 17.

FIG. 18.

FIG. 19.

FIG. 20.

FIG. 17.—PAIR OF STRINGS SET OUT.
FIG 18.—STRINGS TRENCHED FOR WEDGING.
FIG. 19.—TEMPLATE FOR MARKING TRENCHINGS.
FIG. 20.—STRINGS TRENCHED FOR NAILING ONLY.

down when fixing. Thus, if the mark K is the proper limit, the strings should be cut off at L.

Fig. 17 shows the complete pair of strings after

setting out, and it will be seen that some spare material is left at the top ends as well as at the bottom, and in some cases more will be required Here, as will appear hereafter.

The general rule in putting stairs together is to cut out the trenches in the strings to a wedge shape, as in Fig. 18, either making the back cut by guess, which is bad, or using a template (as Fig. 19) to mark them by, which is good, as all the wedges may be cut alike, and they will all fit—a very necessary condition, but one seldom complied with. Another method of trenching is to cut out to the thickness of the treads and risers, fastening these in by nailing. This is very good, providing that each tread and

FIG. 21.   FIG. 22.

FIG. 21.—SECTION OF TREAD AND RISERS : WRONG METHOD.
FIG. 22.—SECTION OF TREAD AND RISERS : RIGHT METHOD.

riser is made to fit tightly in position ; if not, it is very bad. The strings as trenched by the latter method are shown in Fig. 20. (Detailed instructions in this will follow in the next chapter.)

There is also more than one method of bringing the treads and risers together. In Fig. 21 the riser stands on the tread, which is nailed up into the former, while in Fig. 22 the tread fits up to the front of riser, the latter being nailed into the back edge of the former. Of these two methods the latter is much the best, for obvious reasons. Again, in Fig. 21, the tread is grooved on the under side, the riser being tongued into it ; this is good if the treads are thick, as in high-class stairs, but if made from 1-in. stuff only the groove is a source of weakness.

It will, no doubt, be remarked that the width of tread given is very small. Quite true. When the ⅞ in. is added for the nosing, we have only 6 ins., and this is very little ; but how to alter it is the question. We have to get up to a certain height, and have only a certain space to do it in ; thus we cannot have an easier slope, but by having a less number of steps we can get wider treads, and also, we must remember, wider risers as well.

This is shown in Figs. 23 to 25. The first of these is the step we have been working to ; the second gives the result if one step less is used—that is,

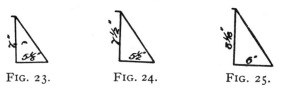

FIG. 23.   FIG. 24.   FIG. 25.

FIGS. 23, 24, AND 25.—COMPARATIVE RISE AND GOING OF STAIRS, AS DESCRIBED, WITH ONE STEP LESS IN NUMBER, AND WITH TWO STEPS LESS IN NUMBER, RESPECTIVELY.

13 treads and 14 risers ; while the third, which gives us a tread of 6 ins., or, including the projecting nosing, of practically 7 ins., and an 8-in. (full) riser results from reducing the number of steps by one more.

It will be noticed that in all these the slope of the string remains the same, and this cannot be altered in the present style of stairs. It is, however, quite possible to so alter the arrangement that an easier stairs may be obtained in the same space, and this we will show how to do in the next chapter.

So far nothing has been said concerning the preparation of the treads and risers. We will, however, deal with this before going further, and it will be as well to give a specification of the stairs we are working on, which, as they are purely for cottage use, should be as follows : Strings—out of 9 by 1½-in. yellow deal ; treads—1-in. yellow deal ; and risers—¾-in. yellow deal.

The treads and risers must be squared off correctly to the length required, as, if not cut square the stairs will be at fault. The former must be planed truly on one side, the front edge rounded for nosing, also planed on the under side about 2 ins. from the nosing, and preferably gauged to a thickness at the same time. They must also be gauged to the width required—in the present case, 6 ins. The risers require planing on one side only, the top edge being planed straight. They may also be cut roughly to 7 ins. wide—that is, the width of the riser plus the thickness of tread.

Next chapter, in addition to showing how the present stairs may be improved, we will show how to finish them, adopting the method shown in Fig. 20. The general method shown in Fig. 18 we will reserve for better stairs, for which it is necessary, and the jerry-builder's method mentioned above we shall not include in this book, as not being worthy of attention.

We would recommend all who wish to learn to make stairs, to construct a model of each type, to about quarter scale, as this will greatly assist them to grasp the methods of working, and will prove far more useful than any amount of descriptive writing.

CHAPTER III

A Cottage Staircase, with Sunk Landing

WE will now show how a staircase of easier pitch may be fitted into the space at disposal, as shown in Chap. II. But before commencing this, we would point out that the general remedy for such a situation would be to make the stairs with winders at the bottom. This would certainly solve the difficulty,

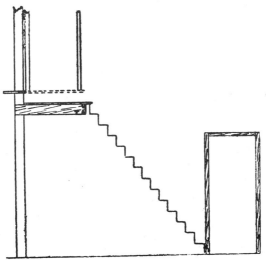

FIG. 26.—SECTIONAL ELEVATION OF STAIRS WITH SUNK LANDING.

but we have a strong prejudice against winding stairs as being expensive, dangerous, and inconvenient; so that, while admitting the necessity of such stairs in certain places, and thus giving them a place later on in the book, we maintain that they should be avoided if possible; and that it is possible in the present case, the following instructions will show.

We are now working to the same measurements as stated in the previous chapter—that is, 8 ft. 9 ins. rise by 6 ft. going, which gives a somewhat steep stairs. Now, to avoid this, or, strictly speaking, to improve on this, instead of allowing the stairs to run up the whole height, as in Fig. 13 (Chap. II), we form what is called a sunk landing (as in Fig. 26 herewith), thus gaining one step in height and having the same going to work on, which means that we require one less rise to take us up to the required height, and allows us to make each tread so much the wider. For instance, in the stairs shown in Fig. 13 (Chap. II) the rise is 7 ins. and the going $5\frac{1}{8}$ ins.,

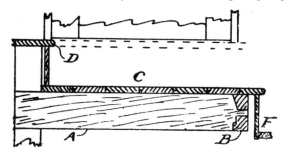

FIG. 27.—PARALLEL SECTION OF SUNK LANDING.

but by reducing the height from 8 ft. 9 ins. to 8 ft. 2 ins. we get fourteen risers of 7 ins. each and thirteen treads of $5\frac{1}{2}$ ins. each; thus, the step-board will be 7 ins. rise by $5\frac{1}{2}$ ins. going.

As the rise of 7 ins. is comparatively low, we may still further improve the stairs by reducing the number of steps—say, instead of fifteen risers, we take thirteen as our requirements, this gives us a rise of 8 ins.; and, as the landing takes off one of these, we have a rise for the actual stairs of 8 ft. 1 in., and for this we shall require eleven treads only, which gives us a going of $6\frac{5}{8}$ ins. bare; or, including the nosing, a tread of $7\frac{1}{2}$ ins. wide, making an easy-going stairs.

We mention this here ; but, for the sake of illustration, Fig. 26 is drawn to show the same rise as
Fig. 13, Chap. II.

Before proceeding with the stairs, we will give
some particulars of the method of forming the sunk
landing. If the stairs pass up between the two
walls, it is easy to throw in the necessary joists
across from wall to wall, but the better plan is to
throw the trimmer across from wall to wall, the
joists themselves to run in a line with the stairs.
This method is also the best to adopt when the

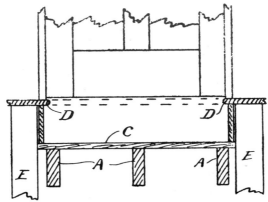

FIG. 28.—CROSS SECTION OF SUNK LANDING.

stairs are fitted to one wall only, the free end of the
trimmer being in this case supported by an upright
piece of timber, which will form a portion of the
wood partition, if such is used to divide off the stairs
from the room.

A section of the sunk landing, parallel with the
stairs, is given in Fig. 27, and a cross-section in
Fig. 28, in each of these A represents the joists,
B the trimmer, C the landing floor, D the main
floor, E the walls between which the stairs are to be
fixed, and F the top step of the stairs as fixed.

These few remarks having, we trust, made clear

what a sunk landing really is, we can proceed with the finishing of the stairs, taking into account that the whole of the materials were planed up in the

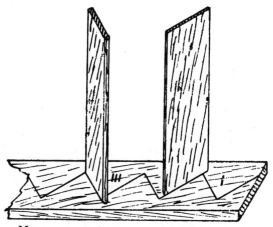

FIG. 29.—METHOD OF MARKING IN TREADS AND RISERS.

previous chapter and the strings set out by means of the step-board.

In Fig. 29, then, we show the method of marking in the treads and risers; in practice, both strings would be laid on the bench as a pair, that is, the bottom ends to the right, thus bringing the top or face edges one towards the worker and the other as far away as possible.

FIG. 30.—STRING AFTER TREADS AND RISERS ARE MARKED IN.

The bottom riser is first taken, standing it on end in the exact position it has to occupy, and marking it in with a marking point; it is then reversed, and the other string marked in the same way. The whole are marked in a similar manner, risers and treads alternately, numbering them as they are marked, as in Fig. 29, until when finished the string appears as Fig. 30. The trenches must now be cut

FIG. 31.—STRING TRENCHED AND BORED FOR RAILS.

out to the uniform depth of $\frac{1}{2}$ in., which operation is best performed by boring a series of holes between all the lines, and then cutting out with a sharp chisel, finishing the fronts of the trenches with a gouge, and finally correcting the depth with the router (" old woman's tooth "). The high speed electric router now makes light of what was once a long and tedious job. Its use is, of course, preferred if available but it must ever be borne in mind that the basic essential for good, sound work is careful and accurate setting out—an electric router used with little thought only allows mistakes and bad work to be produced much more quickly. After trenching, a series of holes should be made in each trench with a suitable sized bradawl, as Fig. 31, thus greatly facilitating the nailing together of the stairs. The holes should be sloped in the direction of the trenches, so that when the strings are nailed to the treads and risers, the nails take positions as in section (Fig. 32).

To put the stairs together, lay one string on the bench, place all the risers and treads in their respective trenches, driving them home ; then lay the other string on top and guide each piece into position one by one, driving the string on gradually, and when home (not before) nail firmly. After nailing on the first string, turn the whole over carefully, so that the bottom string will not slip off, and nail this in the same way ; after which, nail the treads to the risers at the front, and the risers to the treads at the back. If properly done, the stairs will now be

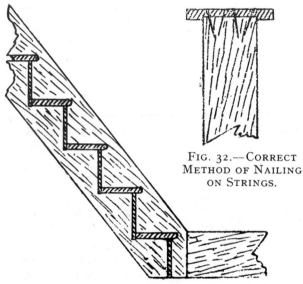

FIG. 32.—CORRECT METHOD OF NAILING ON STRINGS.

FIG. 33.—STAIR STRING INTERSECTING WITH SKIRTING.

very strong, exactly square, and out of twist, and also they will not creak.

To fix the stairs, place in position, scribe down the bottom riser and the strings, cutting the latter upright, so that they will intersect with the skirting, as in Fig. 33. At the top, cut the strings so that they take a bearing against the trimmer, as in Fig. 34, and allowing them to run up so that they intersect with the skirting also, as shown ; or, if preferred, the skirting may be eased off to meet the string, as in Fig. 35, and as an alternative in Fig. 36.

Although the strings can always be made to inter-sect with the skirting in the width, they will not do so in thickness, the one being probably $\frac{1}{2}$ in. thicker than the other, the extra thickness may be eased off as a chamfer, but the better way is to run a thin capping up the strings, scribing it to the wall, as

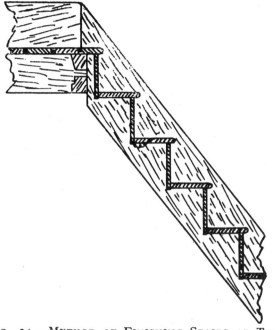

Fig. 34.—Method of Finishing Stairs at Top.

in Fig. 37, continuing it down the front of the skirting, as in Fig. 38. This gives a finished ap-pearance, sufficient for common stairs ; for better ones, of course, we shall make provision later on.

It will be noticed that in Fig. 37 the string is shown as being away from the wall. This should be so, as, if made to fit tightly between walls, there is a great difficulty in getting the stairs in.

We have passed over the fixing of the stairs somewhat lightly, the actual fixing required being very

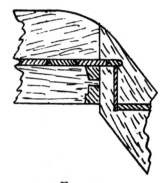
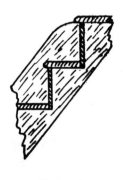

FIG. 35.
ALTERNATIVE METHOD OF
FINISHING AT TOP.

FIG. 36.
FURTHER ALTERNATIVE
METHOD OF FINISHING AT TOP

little, three or four pairs of folding wedges may be
inserted between the strings and walls at intervals,
and nails driven through the strings and wedges into
the walls ; the strings at the top may be nailed to

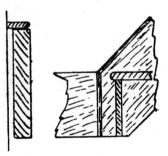

FIG. 37.   FIG. 38.

FIG. 37.—SECTION SHOWING CAPPING FITTED ON TOP OF
STRING.
FIG. 38.—ELEVATION OF FIG. 37, SHOWING CAPPING CON-
TINUED DOWNWARDS.

the trimmer joist and the top riser blocked firmly
and nailed to the same.

CHAPTER IV

A Cottage Staircase with Winders at the Bottom

Winding staircases should in all cases be avoided if possible, on account of certain inconveniences connected with them. But at certain times it so

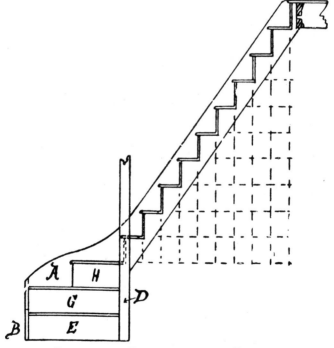

Fig. 39.—Sectional Elevation of Staircase, with Winders at Bottom.

happens that there is no way of getting up to the necessary height without the use of winders, and although these special cases are the result of bad planning as a rule, yet the fact remains that a winding staircase will answer the purpose and no other, hence the necessity of knowing how to form such when the need arises.

We have heard it stated that there is no gain in using winders, but this is most absurd, as anyone who has the least idea of staircasing will agree.

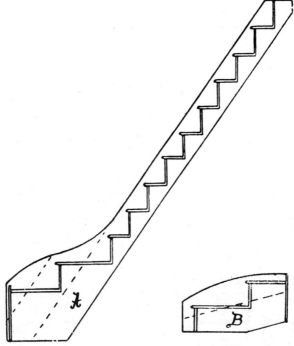

FIG. 40.—PLAN OF FIG. I.

There will, however, be no harm in explaining just where the gain comes in, which we will do, with the assistance of the sectional elevation, Fig. 39 herewith. In this case we have to make a staircase taking us up to the height of 8 ft. 9 ins., the going being only 4 ft. 6 ins. ; thus, if we have a rise of about 8 ins., we get thirteen risers, requiring the going to be divided into twelve treads of $4\frac{1}{2}$ ins., or, including the nosings, each tread would be $5\frac{1}{2}$ ins. only in width, which would not do at all.

Now, by using three winders at the bottom, we get up to the height of 2 ft. without using up any of our going, thus leaving ten risers only, or nine treads to be divided into the 4 ft. 6 ins., giving a tread of 6 ins., or, including the nosings, practically 7 ins., making a passably easy stairway.

The preparation of strings, risers and treads will be the same as for the stairs previously described (in. Chaps. II and III), so we will pass that over, also the setting out and making of the step-board,

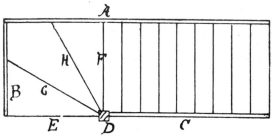

FIG. 41.—WALL STRING AND CONTINUATION.

confining our whole attention to the winding portion at the bottom.

The wall string A (Fig. 41) has to be widened out to carry the extra width of the treads, also continued at right angles for the same purpose, as at B. The complete wall string is shown in Fig. 40, trenched for treads and risers, and the continuation is shown in B. The two may be simply nailed together at the angle, or they may be trenched as shown ; or, if preferred, dovetailed, but the trenching is as good as any.

The right-hand string, C (Fig. 41), is required for the straight part of the stairs only, and is tenoned at the bottom end to fit into the newel D. This

latter may either be of such a length as to take the
handrail only, if the stairs are to be left open at
the side, or if to be closed up the newel may reach
to the ceiling, forming a portion of the partition;
and if a stair foot door is fitted the newel will form
a portion of the door frame. The bottom end of the
newel is trenched to take the treads and risers, as

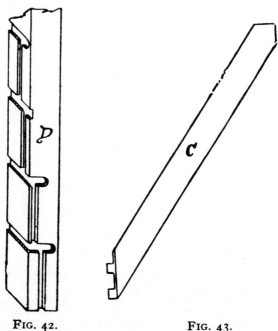

FIG. 42.   FIG. 43.

FIG. 42.—BOTTOM PART OF NEWEL TRENCHED.
FIG. 43.—SHORT STRAIGHT STRING, TENONED TO FIT NEWEL.

in Fig. 42, also mortised to take the short string
(Fig. 43)

It is evident that to ensure perfect fitting, the
mortising and trenching of the newel, also of the
widened strings, and the shaping of the treads and
risers in the winding portion, must be exact, and to
obtain this exactness this part of the stairs should

be set out in plan to the full size, either on the shop floor or on a platform made for the purpose. This plan is shown to a large scale in Fig. 44.

The first riser, E, and the first one in the straight part of the stairs, F, are at right angles to each other, both coming nearly central in the newel; and in order to get the treads almost equal in width, the dotted circle is struck and the width evened out on this, working to the front of the riser in all cases.

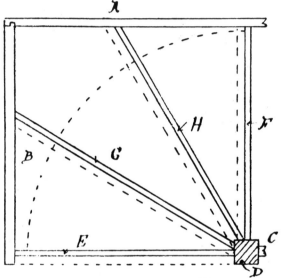

FIG. 44.—WORKING PLAN OF WINDERS.

The dotted straight lines show the front edges of the treads.

After glueing up the strings and treads, the setting out is done with the step-board, continuing the going line to the necessary width of tread, as shown on the plan in each case; the risers will be the same as in the straight part. The lengths and bevels of the treads and risers are also taken from the plan, also the trenchings in the newel.

The ends of the two risers, G and H, will have to be bevelled off to make them fit into the trenches made for them, the first at the back and front, at the right- and left-hand ends respectively, the second *vice versa*. The treads will also be cut on the bevel,

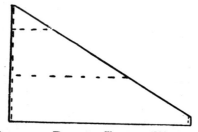

FIG. 45.—BOTTOM TREAD (WINDER).

according to the plan. In many cases the above two risers are not inserted into the newel at all, but simply nailed on. This facilitates putting together, as the stairs can be finished and these two risers inserted after ; but the trenching is the best, although there is some little difficulty in getting all parts into position.

The most ready way of putting together is to first

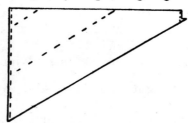

FIG. 46.—TOP TREAD (WINDER)

do the straight portion, then put on the newel and fix with pins, build in the winders downwards, and, lastly, work on the short string B. The treads and risers should not be nailed until all is together. No doubt need be felt as to the parts fitting, if the plan is worked to exactly ; each is bound to fit, while, if otherwise, a good job cannot be made.

We are assuming that the flight of stairs is being made by the method of marking in each tread and riser, no wedges being used, this method being the best for common work, although the stairs will go together somewhat more easily if the treads and risers are wedged. This method will be described in connection with a better class of stairs later on.

In Figs. 45 and 46 we show the first and third winding tread. The grain should in all cases run parallel with the front nosing, as indicated by the dotted lines in Fig. 46, not as Fig. 45. It will be noticed that the nosing on the latter dies out on the front of the newel, and is not trenched in. In extreme cases four winders may be used, but this brings the treads very narrow, and three, as shown in the drawings, are much to be preferred.

CHAPTER V

Staircases with Winders in Middle and at Top

In the previous chapter we described in detail the method of setting out and making a staircase with winders at the bottom, by far the most usual form. We now show how to form the stairs with the winders

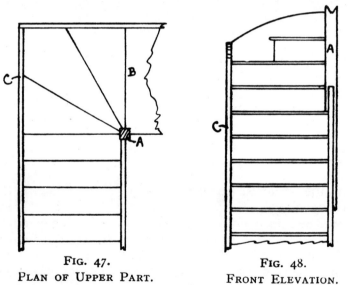

FIG. 47.
PLAN OF UPPER PART.

FIG. 48.
FRONT ELEVATION.

at the top—which is a matter of convenience, and also with them in the middle—which is considered to be artistic.

Although the making of winders at the top does not come so easy as at the bottom, yet the method of setting out and making is exactly the same in both, thus we have not repeated the instructions for making the full-sized plan, etc., which may be taken from the previous chapter. We, however, show in Fig. 47 the plan of the upper part of the stairs with the three winders framed into the newel A, this being fixed to the corner of the landing B. Whether the newel stops at the bottom of the stair string or continues to the floor below, is a matter to be arranged according to circumstances, and is immaterial as regards the making of the stairs. The front elevation (Fig. 48) shows it running down to the floor. This latter drawing shows the return string curved, so as to finish under the top

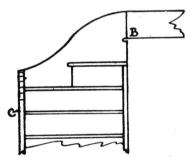

FIG. 49.—STRING MEETING SKIRTING.

nosing—that is, under the landing floor, which is the readiest way, the skirting along the landing being returned on itself, forming a finish quite independent of the stairs. The better way, however, is to curve the string as in Fig. 49, so that it intersects with, and forms a continuation of, the skirting, the joint between the two coming just on the landing as shown.

Fig. 50 shows the wall string C eased off as required at the top, also eased off at the under side, this being, as a rule, necessary on account of the under part being seen.

It may be well to say a few words in explanation

of the necessity of winders at the top of a staircase, otherwise it may be thought that the case shown in Fig. 47 might be met by placing the winders at the bottom and having a level landing at the top. This is quite true, but to have winders at the bottom it is necessary to be able to enter the staircase at right angles to the wall strings, and if unable to do this, we cannot start with winders; therefore, if the height compels us to have winders, and the position of the stairs as regards the other part of the house also confines us to the one way to start them, we

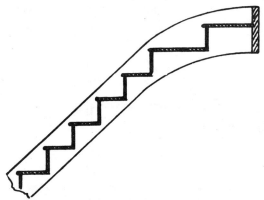

FIG. 50.—SHAPE OF WALL STRING.

must have the winders at the top, where, as a rule, the landing may be arranged satisfactorily.

We now come to what is certainly a more artistic staircase than any of the foregoing, the one with winders in the middle, as shown in plan and elevation in Figs. 51 and 52 respectively. This has some advantages in the small space it occupies, the first part requiring comparatively little going, and by the time the corner is turned, the stairs are sufficiently high to allow of passing under them to other parts of the house.

Such stairs as these are often made with cut strings, moulded treads, etc., also with handrails and balusters ; but as these will be described in future chapters, we pass them over here, dealing with the simple winding staircase only, although

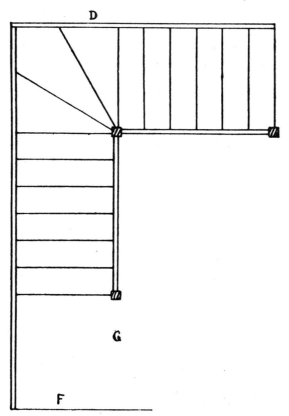

FIG. 51.—PLAN OF STAIRCASE WITH WINDER IN MIDDLE.

we show in Figs. 51 and 52 newels at top and bottom.

In making this staircase, the bottom wall string is eased off as Fig. 54, being widened out as required, and the top wall string D has to be widened

out on the upper side as **Fig.** 53, afterwards continuing the curve from the angle. This is also
eased off at the underside at times; but it is much
better to leave it intact, as in **Fig.** 53, the stairs
being stronger owing to the grain not being cut
on the cross so much.

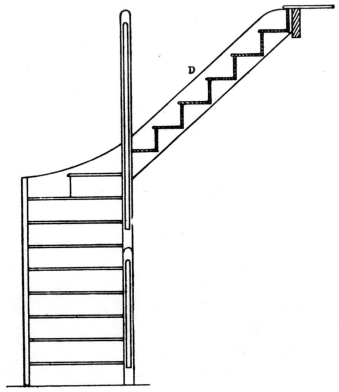

FIG. 52.—ELEVATION OF FIG. 51.

The bottom wall string is widened out at the top
side, as in **Fig.** 54, at E, so that it can be eased out
to meet the skirting, this method of finishing having
a better appearance than making an abrupt joint
between the two.

The elevation of this staircase (Fig. 52) shows the newels at the bottom and at the winding part. These in an ordinary enclosed stairs would run from floor to floor, forming the necessary fixing for the enclosing partition, also the door posts, should the door be at the side. With this style of stairs, however, it is immaterial whether the approach is at the side, as in Fig. 51, or from the front as F, the opening G to be closed up.

The method of putting either of these staircases together is the same as previously described, the one

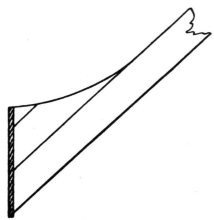

FIG. 53.—METHOD OF WIDENING WALL STRING.

with the winders at the top being much the easier to do. If this is made on a building, the newel may be made the full length, and fixed directly in position ; but if made in the shop, it is much more convenient to make it in two pieces, the splice to come some 10 ins. to 12 ins. below the stairs. This makes the complete staircase more compact, and also takes away the risk of fracturing the newel at the junction with the winders, by an unlucky blow or fall.

The other staircase, if made at the shop, is best

left in two parts, the middle winder being left loose, until in position, as it is a very unwieldy affair if made complete. In many places it would also be

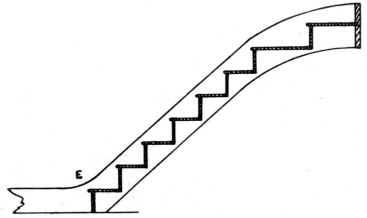

FIG. 54.—LOWER WALL STRING.

difficult to get it in position for fixing. The above remarks concerning the splicing of the newel also apply in this case.

CHAPTER VI

THE DOUBLE FLIGHT OR DOG-LEG STAIRS

HITHERTO we have dealt with only the more common style of stairs, as used in cottage property, but now we come to a different style altogether, made in a different way. The only parts which remain the same as have been already described are the taking of the measurements and the setting out.

As may be judged from the plan of the dog-leg stairs, shown in Fig. 55, these take up considerably more room than any we have dealt with before, not only requiring the space of the first flight, which starts at A and ends at the landing B, but also an equal space in width for the second flight, which starts from C and ends on the floor above at D.

There is, however, a certain amount of space gained in the going, especially if the two flights are made equal in length, or nearly so. Whether this can be done or not depends upon the ground plan of the house; in many cases this is so arranged that a doorway is formed under the second flight, leading to the back part of the house, and this is the way we have shown it in the drawings, the doorway being at E, Fig. 56, and this, of course, makes it necessary to have the first flight sufficiently long to carry us up to the height of some $7\frac{1}{2}$ ft.

The landing should be placed at a height to suit the stairs, so that the rise comes the same in each flight; thus it is best to leave the landing entirely until the stairs are set out, then put it in to suit. The formation of the landing haphazard, and making the stairs after, has been the cause of many other wise good staircases being entirely spoilt.

To revert to the plan (Fig. 55) again, the bottom of the string is tenoned into the newel F, which also

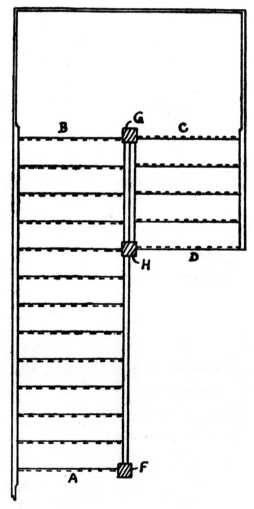

FIG. 55.—PLAN OF DOG-LEG STAIRS.

takes the handrail. At the top of the first flight is the newel G, into which the string is also tenoned

and also the string of the return flight, the top end
of this also being tenoned into the newel H.

In some cases the two strings are in the same
plane, one exactly over the other, but we prefer to

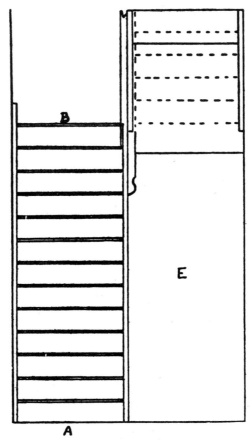

FIG. 56.—ELEVATION OF DOG-LEG STAIRS.

place them so as to just miss each other, one on each
side of a centre line, as in Fig. 55.

The making of the step-board, the setting out of
the strings, and the method of tenoning these to

the newels is the same as has already been described, and need not be repeated ; but the bringing of the two strings to the one newel makes matters more complicated, as they have to be made to come correctly with the step-board.   We show in Fig. 57 the two strings attached to the newel, with the steps set out on both, which should make matters plain, while in Fig. 58 we give a part elevation of the newel, mortised to take the strings, and in Figs. 59

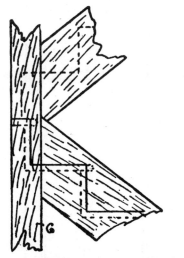

FIG. 57.—ELEVATION OF NEWEL WITH
TWO STRINGS ATTACHED.

FIG. 58.—FRONT OF
NEWEL, SHOWING
MORTISES.

and 60 we show isometric sketches of the newel, the one with the mortises for both strings, and the trenches for the top riser of the bottom flight, and the nosing of the landing, made.   The other is turned halfway round, so as to show the same mortises, and the trenches for bottom riser and tread of the second flight cut out.

Not only have we a different style of stairs this time, but we are putting them together by a different method. Previously the treads and risers have been fitted into the strings tightly, and simply nailed together, but the present treads and risers are securely wedged into the strings, as well as nailed, the wedges being glued also.

This method of trenching makes no difference to

FIG. 59.   FIG. 60.

FIG. 59.—PORTION OF NEWEL MORTISED AND TRENCHED
FOR BOTTOM FLIGHT.

FIG. 60.—PORTION OF NEWEL MORTISED AND TRENCHED
FOR UPPER FLIGHT.

the setting out of the strings as far as the use of the step-board is concerned, but, instead of marking in each tread and riser separately, they are not marked in at all, a template, as Fig. 61, being used instead, the narrow end of which is equal to the thickness of tread or riser, as the case may be, thus the string when set out appears as Fig. 62, the lines marked I being the front of riser and top of tread, as marked from the step-board, the other lines as marked by the template. The string, after the trenches are cut out, appears as Fig. 63.

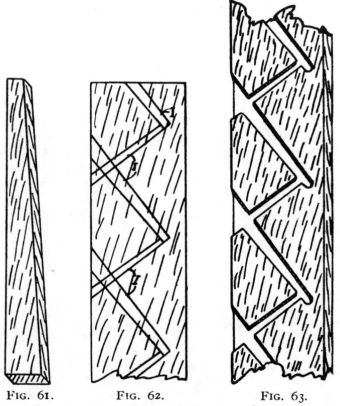

FIG. 61.   FIG. 62.   FIG. 63.

FIG. 61.—TEMPLATE FOR MARKING TRENCHES.
FIG. 62.—PORTION OF STRING WITH TRENCHES MARKED.
FIG. 63.—PORTION OF STRING WITH TRENCHES CUT.

Some men cut the trenches by guess instead of using the template, but this necessitates the fitting of every wedge, or there is a risk of the wedges not having their full holding power ; by using the template, and cutting all wedges alike, no fitting is required.

When cutting out the back part of the trenches, they should be cut slightly under, so as to counteract any tendency of the wedges to draw out when they

FIG. 64.—SECTION OF TREAD WEDGED INTO STRING.

are being driven, it being understood that to fulfil their part properly they must fit closely at all parts, as in Fig. 64.

In such stairs as we are now dealing with, the risers should be tongued up into the treads, as in Fig. 65, and the back edges of the treads into the risers, as in Fig. 66. Do not make the mistake of tongueing both edges of the risers, so that at the

FIG. 65.—RISER TONGUED   FIG. 66.—TREAD TONGUED
INTO TREAD.   INTO RISER.

back of each tread the joint comes as Fig. 67, as this is very bad construction. A small moulding is often fixed under the nosing of the treads, and in this case, the moulding may fit in the groove, and the riser be fixed at the back of it, as in Fig. 68, or the riser may be tongued up into the tread as well. In any case, about four angle blocks, as K, should be glued along the joint of each step.

The putting together of such a staircase as we are

FIG. 67.—WRONG METHOD OF
ATTACHING TREAD TO RISER.

FIG. 68.—TREAD WITH
MOULDING UNDER.

describing is somewhat difficult if done in the ordinary way, the wide trenches having no holding power on the separate treads and risers. The better way to put them together is to first glue and nail all the steps—that is, each tread and its corresponding riser. When the glue is dry, they will stand in

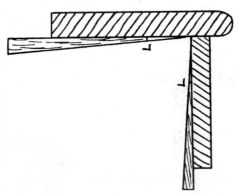

FIG. 69.—DETAIL OF FITTING OF WEDGES.

position by their own weight and can be wedged into the strings without any trouble.

One point in regard to the wedging we have left till now intentionally ; it will be noticed in Fig. 69

that the wedges are seemingly tight, and yet they stop at the points L. This is how they should fit ; if made so that they reach to the ends of the trenches, the probability is that they will be tight endways before they are sideways, which is what we do not want ; whereas, if made as shown, they can be driven in to any extent without becoming bound at the ends.

It will be found necessary to wedge all the risers (or treads) first, then to cut off the surplus ends of the wedges before the treads (or risers) can be wedged, but this is only a detail and easily got over. Do not be niggardly in the use of the glue on the wedges, as what squeezes out at the sides helps to hold, and it acts as a safeguard against damp.

CHAPTER VII

"Cut" or "Open" String Stairs

A "cut" string staircase is one where the string which does not come close up to the wall (the wall string) is cut to the outline of the several steps, the risers being mitred to the cut part, and the treads

FIG. 70.—ELEVATION OF CUT STRINGS, WITH TREADS IN POSITION.

cut so as to nail direct on the string, the nosings on the tread being continued longer and mitred, so that return nosings can be nailed on to the ends of the treads and returned on themselves at the opposite ends. There can be no question as regards the appearance of a cut string staircase being far superior

to any other, but owing to the extra work involved
in the construction, this form of stairs has, in some
localities, fallen into disrepute, but it is equally
certain that it will come into fashion again at some
time, as it fully deserves to do.

The setting out of a cut string staircase is the
same as for those we have already described, as indeed is the construction, to a certain extent, the
alterations being wholly connected with the one

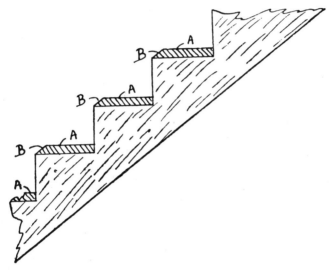

FIG. 71.—PORTION OF STRING, SHOWING MITRES TO TAKE
RISERS.

string, and the ends of the treads and risers which
fix to it.

It will be remembered that in an ordinary closed
string staircase, the strings are set out as a pair,
the trenching coming on the inside of each ; this
latter applies to the wall string of the present stairs,
but the other one must be set out on the *outside*.
Thus, instead of pairing with the wall string, it is,
when set out, exactly like it. One other point in

connection with this setting out. The marks, as made from the step-board, show the front of the riser and the top of the tread, and as the treads nail flat on to the string where it is cut, other marks must be made the thickness of the treads below those already made. The reason for this can be seen by glancing at Fig. 70, which represents the string with the treads nailed on.

In setting out the wall string, the housing marks

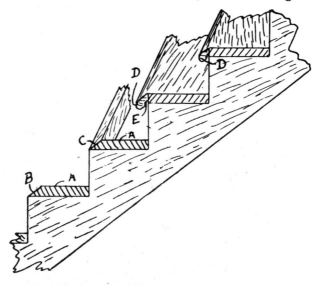

FIG. 72.—SHOWING FIXING OF RISERS AND TREADS.

are made a certain distance from the upper edge of the string; but with the cut string this should not be done, as it would only mean the wasting of a certain amount of wood.

We can now consider the string as set out ready for cutting. In doing the latter, the seating for the treads should be done first, making it at right angles with the side of the string as A, Fig. 71. After cutting in for the treads, the riser seatings can be cut, but these must be made so that the risers will mitre to them, as B. The angles should be such as to make the riser and string intersect exactly, as at C, Fig. 72, and in plan in Fig. 73 ; and as the

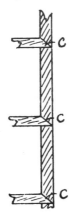

FIG. 73.—PLAN OF STRING, WITH RISERS FIXED.

former will probably be 1 in. thick, and the latter ½ in. more, they will not come to what is usually considered a true mitre, that is, 45 degs.

All the seatings cut out, the string has the appearance of Fig. 71, and in Fig. 72 is shown the various

FIG. 74.—PLAN OF TREAD, MITRED FOR RETURN AND MORTISED FOR BALUSTERS.

stages of putting together; but this is somewhat anticipating matters.

The risers must all be cut off to the exact length, always remembering that instead of allowing the

$\frac{1}{2}$ in. to enter the string, in this case we require length enough to reach to the outside of the same. The ends which come to the cut string must be cut cleanly to the proper angle as before described. The treads must be cut off square to the same length

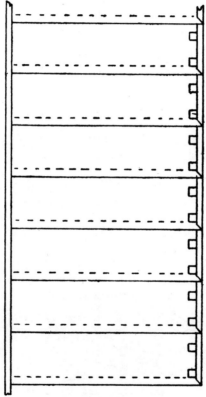

FIG. 75.—PLAN OF STAIRS—DOTTED LINES SHOW FRONT OF RISERS.

as the risers, with the exception of the nosings, which should project, and be cut into the form of a mitre, as at D, Fig. 72, also shown in plan in Fig. 74. Grooves should also be made on the under side to take the moulded fillets in front of the risers, as E,

Fig. 72. Before the treads are fixed, the mortises should be made for the balusters to fit in, as F, Fig. 74 ; these must be set out so that they will come equal distances between, up the stairs, as in Fig. 75.

In putting the stairs together, each step should be made complete in itself first, not only nailed, but glued and blocked, and allowed to dry, then wedged into the wall string, and, lastly, the cut string nailed

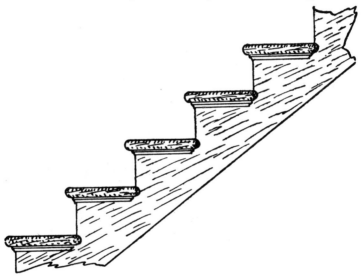

FIG. 76.—STAIRS, WITH RETURNS FIXED.

on, and blocked underneath, the returns to the nosings being nailed on after, which finishes the stairs, the side appearance then being as Fig. 76.

The above is the most simple form of open string stairs. A more elaborate form is that shown in Fig. 77, where, by the addition of the shaped brackets, the work is given a much more finished appearance, while the extra labour is not considerable. The use of the shaped brackets requires some slight alteration in the cutting of the string, as, instead of the risers mitreing to the latter, they will be mitred to the brackets only. Thus the string will be cut square for the risers to fit to, but instead of the latter resting directly against the seating, it is much better to shoulder them and cut the string from $\frac{1}{4}$ in. to $\frac{1}{2}$ in. in front of the mark, as in Fig. 78.

The mitre on the end of the riser must project forward beyond the string the thickness of the brackets, which is, as a rule, $\frac{3}{8}$ in., and the treads

FIG. 77.—STAIRS, WITH SHAPED BRACKETS.

also must be made so much longer, as shown in Fig. 79 (where dotted line shows the outside of string), and Fig. 80, which shows a vertical section of Fig. 77.

In Figs. 81 and 82 we show alternative shapes for brackets, which may be modified to any extent It will be noticed in Fig. 80 that the moulded fillet, which intersects with that under the nosings, is made solid, and not fitted up into the return nosings. The reason is this : if the latter were grooved, instead of the ends to the right in the drawings being rounded on themselves, they would have to be mitred as dotted line in Fig. 79. This is undoubtedly the proper way for the best work, although it is rarely done. If, however, this is done, then the fillet under the returns should fit in grooves in the latter, and the brackets run up to the under side of the treads.

FIG. 78.—SECTION SHOWING RISER MITRED TO TAKE BRACKET.

In Fig. 77 we show a portion of the panelled spandril under the string of the stairs, and the section (Fig. 80) shows the connection between the two. An alternative method is to fit the rail of spandril under the string and plant on a piece of moulding over the joint.

FIG. 79.—PLAN OF TREAD, WITH RETURN FIXED.

We have neither shown nor mentioned the tongueing of the riser into the treads in front, or the tongueing of the treads into the risers at the back, for the simple reason that we described this before, but in stairs of this description it should on no account be omitted. The same also applies to the glueing in of the angle blocks. This should be done in every angle where it is possible to find room for

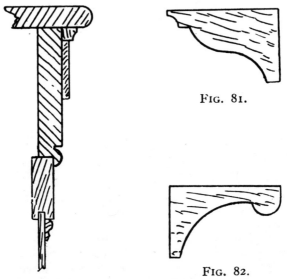

FIG. 81.

FIG. 82.

FIG. 80.—VERTICAL SECTION   ALTERNATIVE SHAPES OF
OF FIG. 77.   BRACKETS.

a block. The fixing together of the complete steps before the actual staircase is built up is best done on a specially made cradle, which will be described in a future chapter.

CHAPTER VIII

Stairs with Continuous Strings

As a rule we find, in continuous string staircases, that the string is cut or open, as described in the previous chapter; but in the present article we show a close string, for the reason that this simplifies matters and avoids repetition. The setting out of the present style of staircase is almost the same as the dog-leg or two-flight, with the exception that, instead of the strings of the bottom and top flight being tenoned into newels at the landing, the string is bent round, as shown in the plan (Fig. 83), and it is the bending of the string, combined with the methods of finding the correct position of the trenching in passing from one part of the stairs to the other, where the whole difficulty lies.

We confess that the making of these stairs is not easy for the novice, but there are no difficulties in them which cannot be surmounted by perseverance and common-sense. A very simple experiment will serve to show the principle of the continuous string. Set out to scale on a piece of paper, or cardboard, an ordinary stair string; then bend this diagonally round a cylinder, the scale diameter of which corresponds with that set out on the paper. If the cylinder be kept vertical, and the lines on the paper kept horizontal, we have an exact fac-simile of a continuous string for our stairs, and half an hour spent in studying this experiment will be well repaid in the knowledge gained thereby.

The plan (Fig. 83) shows a staircase with a 6-in.

well—that is, the distance between the strings of the upper and lower parts of the stairs, which means that the string has to be bent to a circle of 3-in. radius.

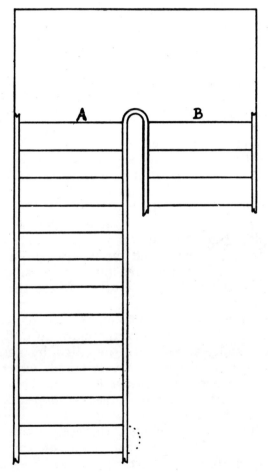

FIG. 83.—PLAN OF CONTINUOUS STRING STAIRCASE.

The string, as set out for this, is shown in Fig. 84, A and B being the last riser of the bottom, and the first of the top flight respectively, as in Fig. 83, the tread line C being the floor of the landing ; thus, it follows that the part between A and B is that which forms the bend, and it must therefore be of the correct length to exactly reach round the half circle.

With a small well-hole, such as we are now dealing with, it is easy to get the necessary length here without interrupting the straight line of the string, the going, as we have set it out, being 8½ ins., and the bending portion only having to be ¾ in. more ; thus, by keeping the nosings of the upper flight

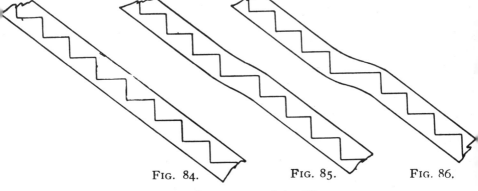

FIG. 84.   FIG. 85.   FIG. 86.

FIG. 84.—STRING FOR 6-IN. WELL.
FIG. 85.—STRING FOR 8-IN. WELL, SHOWING EASEMENT.
FIG. 86.—STRING FOR 10-IN. WELL, SHOWING EASEMENT.

slightly farther from the top of the string than in the bottom flight, we attain our object.

In the case of a larger well, however, the string has to be eased both on top and underneath, as Figs. 85 and 86, which show the easement necessary for 8- and 10-in. wells respectively.

In theory the continuous string can be in one piece quite well, but not so in practice, owing to the impossibility of handling the complete staircase ; thus, it is necessary to have a joint, and this should be made to come nearly close to the curve and on the upper flight, and the best way to manage this is to set out the string so far, make the splicing, and finish setting out as though it was in one.

The setting out finished, the trenching must also be done, and then the bending of the string requires attention. To do this, the string is cut away on the inside, so as to leave only a thin veneer

FIG. 87.—STRING CUT AWAY FOR BENDING ROUND WELL.

on the outside, as Fig. 87, making the cuts to the angle of the risers, as Fig. 88, and cutting away that portion only which has to bend round the well ; thus, the outlines of the cut-away part will be the two riser lines A and B (Fig. 84), and the thickness of the riser A will come into the cut-away part, but not the riser B.

The best way to bend the string is to make a solid block, as Fig. 89, the curve of which is the

FIG. 88.—SHOWING ANGLE OF CUT AWAY PART.

exact size of the well, and the length sufficient to take the whole of the string as it is bent round it diagonally. The thin part of the string must be soaked well with hot water, and then it should bend round easily. To hold it in position, the long part (the bottom flight portion) can be screwed to the block, as at D (Fig. 90), the other end, after being bent round, being also screwed as shown.

To ensure the string fitting tightly to the block—
which is absolutely essential to make a true curve—
a block can be screwed to the halving of the string,

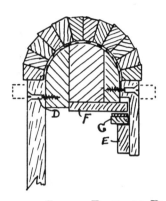

FIG. 89.—BLOCK TO
BEND STRING ROUND.

FIG. 90.—STRING FIXED TO BLOCK,
ALSO FILLED IN ON OUTSIDE.

as E (Figs. 90 and 91), and another one to the main
block, projecting into the halving as F, the folding
wedges G can then be driven in tightly between the
two, and will pull the veneer hard and solid round

FIG. 91.—SECTIONAL ELEVATION OF TIGHTENING
ARRANGEMENT.

the main block. The part of the string which was
cut away must now be replaced in the form of strips,
as shown in Fig. 90, and as these will be held by glue

only, it follows that they must be accurately fitted, and well rubbed into position, using good hot glue.

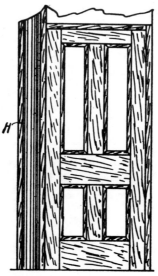

FIG. 92.--SOLID PILLAR UNDER WELL, WITH DOOR FITTED TO SAME.

Should the stairs be of hardwood, to be finished in itself and not painted, the screws which fix the strings to the block may be objected to ; if so, two strips, as dotted lines, may be used, screwing the

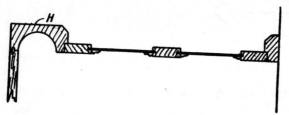

FIG. 93.—SECTIONAL PLAN OF FIG. 92.

ends to the block, so that they hold the string; but this is scarcely as safe as the direct screwing.

After the glue is set, the blocks must be finished off round the curve, making them the same as the string in both width and thickness. It will be found most convenient to do the former first, squaring them from the inside of the well as the work proceeds, and after this is done, the thickness can be gauged round, taking care to finish on the outside smoothly.

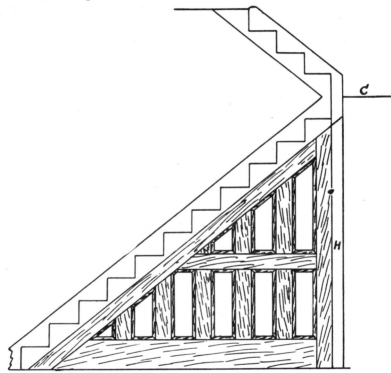

FIG. 94.—SECTIONAL ELEVATION OF STAIRS AND SPANDRIL.

The risers A and B should not be wedged, but fitted closely, and fixed by nailing and blocking only. In a staircase with a well larger than the 6 ins. which we are now describing, it will be inconvenient to make the block (Fig. 89) solid, as shown, but it can easily be built up centre fashion, taking care to work it truly, and fixing the strips closely together ; it will then answer the purpose as well as a solid block.

Should the house be so planned that a door is placed under the landing, the curved well-hole is often continued down to the floor level, in the form of a solid pillar, which not only supports the stairs and landing, but forms the doorpost. This is shown in elevation in Fig. 92, and in sectional plan in Fig. 93, while Fig. 94 shows the elevation (sectional) of the complete stairs, with spandril and landing level, H representing the above-mentioned pillar in each drawing. The fitting of this to the string at the top end is a little intricate, on account of the spiral shape of the latter, but it is best to fit it properly rather than to cut away the string.

Staircases are often made with continuous strings from basement to attic, which, of course, makes the work more complicated, and the measurements have to be very exactly taken and worked to, but the principle remains the same throughout.

CHAPTER IX

BULLNOSE AND CURTAIL STEPS

IN the better class of staircases the bottom step
is often formed as a " bullnose " step, or, more rarely,
as a " curtail " step, both styles undoubtedly adding
greatly to the appearance of the finished staircase.

We propose first to deal with the most commonly
used, and the easiest to do, this being the former.
Why this should be called a " bullnose " step, it

FIG. 95.—SIDE ELEVATION OF BULLNOSE STEP, NEWEL AT
BACK.

is difficult to say, but it probably got the title first
as a term of ridicule, through being substituted for
the more difficult and costly curtail step made
years ago, when the latter was commonly used.

The side elevations of two different styles of stairs
fitted with bullnose steps at the bottom are given
in Figs. 95 and 96. The first is a cut string stair,
with the newel at the back of the tread entirely,
while the second is a close-string stair, with the

newel in the centre of the curved part of the tread ;
and although we show the newel placed differently
in the two styles, there is no reason why the posi-

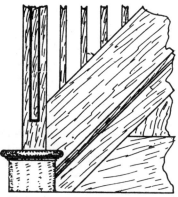

FIG. 96.—SIDE ELEVATION OF BULLNOSE STEP, NEWEL IN
CENTRE.

tions may not be reversed, if preferred, the position
of the newel on the tread having no connection with
the style of the staircase, either being used at will.
Personally, we prefer Fig. 96 to the other, unless

FIG. 97.—FRONT ELEVATION OF BULLNOSE STEP.

there is some special reason for using the position
shown in Fig. 97.

The front elevation of both Figs. 95 and 96 is
as shown in Fig. 97.

We have seen the risers of bullnose steps built up solid, but this is decidedly wrong, the proper method being to build up a solid block, and bend the curved part of the riser round it in the form of thin veneer, and the. doing of this properly comprises practically the whole difficulty in the formation of the step.

In Fig. 98 we give a sectional plan of the bullnose step, with the newel attached as Fig. 95, the inner lines showing the scotia moulding and the front of riser.

The block which forms the foundation of the step is built up as Fig. 99 ; the three (or more) pieces

FIG. 98.—SECTIONAL PLAN   FIG. 99.—BLOCK BUILT UP
OF BULLNOSE STEP.   AND CUT TO SHAPE.

used must be of thoroughly dry and seasoned timber, and the whole must be screwed and glued together firmly.

The radius of the curve depends upon the width of the tread, and in striking it out, allowance must be made for the thickness of the veneer, which should not be more than 3-16ths in. The curved end should be continued on the straight about an inch at the front, and slightly more at the back, the finish of the latter taking the form of a tongue, as shown.

The depth of the recesses at front and back of the block must be the same as the thickness of the riser minus the veneer, so that the solid parts of the riser will bed into the recesses firmly, at the same time as the veneer fits tightly to the circle.

The riser, as cut to fit round the block, is shown in Fig. 100, the short, solid end to the left fitting on to the back of the block, the shoulder being grooved to fit on the tongue made for the purpose.

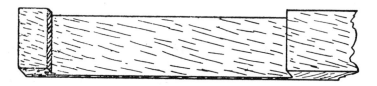

FIG. 100.—RISER CUT FOR BENDING ROUND BLOCK.

The length of the veneer must be such as to reach round the solid part of the block, with about an inch to spare, this spare portion being for the reception of a pair of folding wedges to tighten up the veneer on the block.

To fit the riser on to the block, place the short end in position and fix with about three screws, taking care that the tongue is close up in its groove,

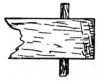

FIG. 101.—RISER SCREWED AND   FIG. 102.—FOLDING
WEDGED TO BLOCK.   WEDGES TIGHTENING
UP RISER.

as in Fig. 101 ; then bend the veneer round steadily until the long end is close to the block, when it can be held temporarily with a small cramp at top and bottom, while the folding wedges are inserted, as in Fig. 102. These must be driven in very gently until the veneer fits the curve all round, but not so tightly as to risk a fracture, the final fixing being by screws through the lug of the block from the inside into the thick part of the riser.

The whole of the above should be done first without using glue, and when all is correctly fitted, the screws and wedges may be removed, the veneer and the block thoroughly wetted with hot water, then glued, and the fixing done again permanently.

It goes without saying that a perfect piece of board must be used for the riser, especially as regards the veneered part. This should then bend round without difficulty. At the same time, should there seem a danger of splitting if it be bent dry, hot

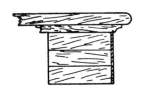 

FIG. 103.—SOLID SCOTIA AND   FIG. 104.—NEWEL
           TREAD.   HOUSED OVER BACK
                                     OF STEP.

water may be used previous to the first fitting. The wetting, as above mentioned, is not to assist in the bending, but to prevent the glue from setting before the parts are in position. These days a great deal of parana pine is used in staircasing. It would be inappropriate to attempt the technique we have just discussed using this timber.

It is necessary that the curved part of the block, also the inside of the veneered part of the riser, be finished as truly and smoothly as though it would be seen in the finished work, otherwise the imperfections will be visible on the outside, and there will also be a risk of splitting the veneer, owing to uneven pressure.

The scotia moulding under the tread is worked on a solid piece of board, the block and riser being cut down to suit, as in Fig. 103, and the tread is also made solid to shape, the nosing being worked round it.

If the newel is fitted in the position shown in Fig. 95, it must be scribed to the back of the step, as Fig. 104 ; but if it has to stand in the middle of the tread, as Fig. 96, the block and the tread must be mortised to receive it (the mortise in the former being shown in Fig. 99). In the first case it will be fixed by screws from the back, while in the second

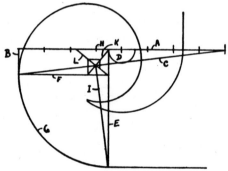

FIG. 105.—METHOD OF STRIKING OUT SCROLL FOR CURTAIL STEP.

it can be wedged from underneath the step. The stair string will in both cases be tenoned in and fixed with pins in the usual way.

We now come to the more complicated curtail step, which, although the method of construction has much in common with the bullnose step, is yet much more difficult to make. The curtail step is really a scroll, and the setting out of this was often a puzzle in the workshop, played off on the younger hands in former days, and possibly it is the same now, though not so often wanted. There are many ways of arriving at the correct result, one of the most simple being that given in Fig. 105, the explanation of which we will give in detail.

On a waste piece of board draw a straight line A, say, for the sake of illustration, 1 ft. long. Divide this into eight equal parts, as shown, square down the length of one part, as B, and make the diagonal line C. From the middle point of line A strike the semicircle D, touching the diagonal, and from the left of the semicircle square down the line E; make F parallel with A until it cuts E, and this gives the point from which to strike the first part of the scroll G. Now square down from point H to

FIG. 106.—BLOCK FOR CURTAIL STEP WITH RISER WEDGED ON.

F, make diagonal I through F on to C, and through the latter point make the two diagonals K and L, connecting these with vertical and horizontal lines, as shown, and these then give the centres from which to strike the remaining arcs of the scroll. It will be found that this method of striking out will give a scroll the width of which will be rather more than two-thirds of the length of line A; thus it is easy to make the required calculations as regards the size.

Fig. 106 shows the block for forming the curtail step, with the riser wedged on it. The block is

built up as described for Fig. 99—in three or more
thicknesses of well-seasoned dry wood, screwed and
glued together, lugs being left on at the front, through
which screws can be inserted into the thick part
of the riser after the veneer is stretched tightly by
the folding wedges, and also at the back, as shown,
by which the block can be securely screwed to the
string of the stairs.

The riser is continued, as veneer, completely round
the scroll, and may be fixed in the throat of same by
inserting the end in a slot made in a round pin, as
shown in Fig. 106, glueing and screwing it before the
pin is passed into the hole made for it in the block;
or what is perhaps the better way, a square mortise

FIG. 107.—CENTRAL BLOCK, WITH VENEER GLUED AND
SCREWED IN.

may be made in the block, the end of the veneer
being fixed in a slot made for it in the square block
to fit in the mortise, as Fig. 107.

Another slot must be made in the central pin
or square block on which the veneer is fixed, which
fits round the concave part of the block, and which
in the finished stairs forms a continuation of the
string; and to ensure a good fit up to the latter,
an inch or so should be allowed beyond the actual
length required, as in Fig. 106.

As this concave veneer cannot be stretched tightly
on the block by wedging, a caul should be fitted,
as shown. This will wedge tightly in the throat of
the scroll, and may be clamped to the lug of the
block by means of the folding wedges, as in Fig. 106.

The scotia moulding and the tread are shaped solid to fit the scroll, in the same way as described in connection with the bullnose step.

These curtail steps are sometimes fitted with a wood newel planted in about the centre of the back part of the scroll ; but, oftener, an iron newel of slighter build is used, and balusters fixed in a cluster round the scroll at gradually widening intervals. In the former case the newel passes through the block

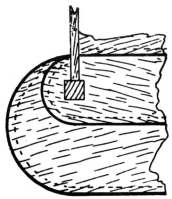

FIG. 108.—PLAN OF DOUBLE BULLNOSE STEP.

of the step, and is wedged from underneath, but in the latter the iron newel is either provided with a screw thread to screw into tread and block, or with thread and nut to screw up from below. Either of these makes a strong job.

In some staircases, where there is plenty of room, and something better than an ordinary bullnose step is wanted, the double bullnose step may be used, and looks very well. A plan of this form of step is shown in Fig. 108, and as it consists simply of one bullnose step mounted on a wider one, no special instructions in making are necessary, beyond stating that the newel should be fixed in the centre of the top step of the two, as shown in the drawing.

CHAPTER X

A High-class Staircase with Square Well and Sunk-Panelled Newels

As a fitting conclusion to this Handbook, we give a design for a staircase for one of the modernised old-style houses now so fashionable, which may be adapted to almost any dimensions, and will be found to look exceedingly well, while the work in making is not excessive, therefore the cost will be kept within reasonable limits.

Such a staircase as this looks best in oak ; English for preference, but Austrian or Riga make good substitutes, while, if good well-seasoned elm can be obtained, it looks very well indeed, but unless extremely well seasoned it will be found to twist and shrink considerably.

The staircase, as shown in plan (Fig. 109), in front elevation (Fig. 110), and in part side elevation (Fig. 111), has a going of eleven and a half feet, and a rise of the same distance, these being divided up into sixteen and seven risers of six inches at the bottom and top flights respectively ; thus the going and height of each step works out at nine and six inches, and makes a very easy stairs.

As shown, the stairs has a double bullnose step at the bottom, the string is " open," and newels are used at the bottom and top of each flight, not only in the open side, but also at the wall side ; these latter being half the thickness only, and fitted with half a handrail as well.

The methods of setting out and building this staircase are identical with those which have been already described; but in one of the previous chapters we mentioned the fact that the better way of

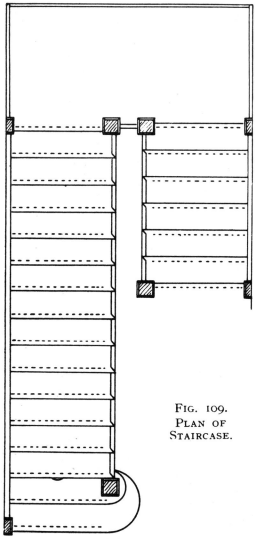

FIG. 109.
PLAN OF
STAIRCASE.

putting together a "cut" or "open" string stairs was, first to glue up each step complete in itself, and

the proper way to do this was to use a " carriage,"
or, rather, two, a description of these carriages being
postponed at the time.

We now show in Fig. 112 a form of carriage for
glueing up the steps on. Two are required, and

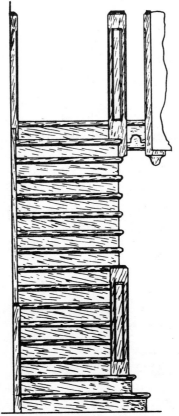

FIG. 110.—FRONT ELEVATION OF STAIRCASE.

they should be screwed to the bench top, at a suitable distance apart, parallel with each other, in
the position as drawn. The scotia is first glued
into its groove, then the tread is laid on the bottom
member of the carriage, and held in place by the

button. The riser is next placed in position, and held there by the top button, while the blocks are glued in the angles, care being taken first to place both tread and riser level at the end, as required for fitting to the strings.

After each tread is glued up, it can be carefully removed and laid aside to dry.

Fig. 113 shows the most suitable section for tread and riser in a stairs of this kind, the scotia and riser having each a separate groove, which is better,

FIG. 111.—PART SIDE
ELEVATION OF STAIRCASE.

FIG. 112.—CARRIAGE FOR
PUTTING TREADS TOGETHER.

though not quite so quickly done as placing them both in one groove. A sketch of the riser, with groove made for tread, and tongue to fit into tread, is given in Fig. 114.

The newels, as shown, are 6 ins. square, moulded round the top, and stop-moulded at the · corners. They are also sunk-panelled on all four sides, the edges of the sunk part being moulded, as shown in the elevation (Fig. 115) and the section (Fig. 116) of the newel.

The framing of the newels to the strings has already been dealt with, but it matters little whether the half newels are fixed to the wall string with mortise and tenon, or fitted over them after the stairs are fixed. Undoubtedly the framing is the most work-

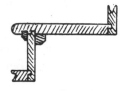

FIG. 113.—SECTION OF ONE COMPLETE STEP.

FIG. 114.—END OF RISER READY FOR FIXING.

manlike method, and the extra time taken to do it is very little.

The newels at the landing should be long enough to come below the ceiling and finish with a drop, as shown in Fig. 110, or, better still, they may be left still longer, and a small arch fitted between, as shown in Fig. 117.

It will be noticed in Fig. 111 that the string is widened out and finished with a curve at the bottom end, also that the spandril, instead of being panelled,

FIG. 115.—ELEVATION OF NEWEL.

is formed of upright boards. This style of finish looks very effective in practice, and can be recommended as something better than the usual way.

Fig. 118 shows the wall string with the half newel and handrail. This latter is omitted in Figs. 109 and 110, for the reason that we are not dealing with

handrailing at present, and if included in the draw·
ings, it would cover up some of the details.

The balusters required for the type of staircase
shown in Fig. 111 would be square in section (1½-in.

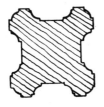

FIG. 116.—SECTION OF   FIG. 117.—FINISH OF NEWEL
NEWEL.   AT WELL.

side), and placed corner-ways. Thus the treads and
nosings, instead of being mortised, have to be cut
out V-shaped to take them. This style is not adopted
for the sake of cheapness, as the balusters cost as
much and take longer to fix than the ordinary turned

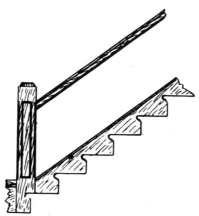

FIG. 118.—ELEVATION OF WALL STRING AND HALF NEWEL.

ones, but these latter are not suited to this style of
staircase.

Should the square balusters be objected to, twisted
ones look very well, though they come somewhat

expensive ; if used, they should not be less than 2 ins. square at top and bottom.

In Fig. 119 we give the shape of the bracket pieces, as shown in Fig. 111, but these have to be modified to suit the particular measurements of the staircase in hand.

We might mention that in a staircase such as the one we are now dealing with, all parts must be of substantial thickness, thus 1½ ins. at least must be used for strings and tread, and 1 in. for the risers ; 2 ins. is really not too much for the strings.

Should the space under the landing be open,

FIG. 119.—SHAPE OF BRACKET.

the two newels of the bottom flight should be connected by an arch, also those at the top of the same flight, similar to Fig. 117, but the arch would, of course, be considerably longer. The drops of the newels must all be of the same length and finished to the same pattern, bringing the arch to such curves as will suit.

With this we come to the end of our Handbook, in which we have dealt with the basic techniques of good quality staircasing and which, we feel, will prove to be the most useful to amateur and professional. Where hot glues have been referred to, their modern counterparts can be employed but care should be taken. Much of the work calls for the rubbed joint and only modern adhesives that lend themselves to this technique should be used.

A complete and thorough study of this Handbook should provide a good working knowledge of elementary staircasing and if, in addition, as suggested elsewhere in these pages, quarter scale models are made up, putting the information included here into practice, then that knowledge will be amply reinforced with practical confidence.

INDEX